REMEMBER

Remember:
God's Covenants and the Cross

Remember

978-1-7910-3020-9

978-1-7910-3021-6 *eBook*

Remember: DVD

978-1-7910-3019-3

Remember: Leader Guide

978-1-7910-3022-3

978-1-7910-3018-6 *eBook*

Also by Susan Robb

Called: Hearing and Responding to God's Voice

Seven Words: Listening to Christ from the Cross

The Angels of Christmas: Hearing God's Voice in Advent

On Purpose: Finding God's Voice in Your Passion
(With Magrey R. de Vega, Sam McGlothlin, and Jevon Caldwell-Gross)

REMEMBER

God's Covenants
and the Cross

SUSAN ROBB

ABINGDON PRESS | NASHVILLE

Remember:
God's Covenants and the Cross

Copyright © 2023 Abingdon Press
All rights reserved.

Library of Congress Control Number: 2023943934
978-1-7910-3020-9

MANUFACTURED IN THE UNITED STATES OF AMERICA

For my sisters in covenant,

Alice, Sue, Cindy,
Beth, Fran, and Elizabeth

CONTENTS

INTRODUCTION

This book explores the relationship between Lent and memory (God's and our own), and especially the season's connection to the covenants in the Bible. While many covenants are mentioned in the Old Testament (also called the Hebrew Scriptures, which were scriptures Jesus knew and cited), there are four major covenants instituted by God. These covenants are foundational to our recognition of the true nature and character of God.

God makes covenants through Noah, Abraham, Moses, and David. These four covenants are also primary to our recognition of who Jesus is, and how these covenants relate to the way in which he lived his life, his journey to the cross, his resurrection, and the institution of what the prophet Jeremiah described in his day as a new covenant. We will see that while Jesus becomes and institutes a new covenant with and for us, this covenant does not replace the others. God does not break one covenant to make another. This new covenant is the fulfillment and pinnacle of the other covenants instituted by God out of love for all of God's creation.

Of course, we all know the relevance of Jesus's journey to the cross and his resurrection as the basis for, and the pinnacle of, our faith as Christians. But if we wish to fully integrate the importance of Jesus's journey to the cross with our own Lenten journey, it's not enough to begin with Jesus's triumphal entry into Jerusalem on Palm Sunday.

We must go back to the beginning, to creation in which "the Word made flesh" who dwelt among us was fully engaged. We must remember that he spoke, and all things came into being through him, and without him not one thing came into being (John 1:3).

Introduction

We must remember what Jesus himself, as one who was fully human and fully divine, remembered—what he, as a devout Jew and Creator, would have remembered about the salvation history of Israel, the world, and all of creation. What we will soon discover is that when God remembers God's people, deliverance and salvation begin. And when God remembers us, we are then asked to remember what God has done for us, especially in this season of Lent.

> *When God remembers God's people, deliverance and salvation begin. And when God remembers us, we are then asked to remember what God has done for us, especially in this season of Lent.*

I've confessed in the past that, before I became a minister in a church that valued the liturgical seasons of the Christian calendar, I loved to go from the joy of Palm Sunday to the joy of Easter morning. Or, to hear the story of the birth of Jesus and the songs of the angels, without hearing of the death threats of Herod and their foreshadowing of the cross. My desire was to go from joy to joy and avoid the unpleasantness of Jesus's betrayal, arrest, torture, and crucifixion.

However, after leading many services during the Advent, Christmas, Lent, and Easter seasons, I became aware of how engaging fully in the rituals and Scriptures of these seasons helps us better understand the Incarnation, Resurrection, and our own salvation history. More than that, fully engaging in the liturgical rituals and Scripture of each season and understanding their background and importance bring depth and richness to our faith, to our relationship with God and Jesus Christ, and to our relationship with and responsibility toward others in the world and the whole of creation itself—a richness we could never know otherwise.

During my last two years in ministry at Highland Park United Methodist Church in Dallas, I was given the honor of serving as the pastor to its Cox Chapel community. This service within the church is famously known for being steeped in liturgy and the sacraments. My favorite two services of the year are the Lessons and Carols service, held just before Christmas, and the Easter Vigil service held the night before Easter morning. One element I love about these services is that no sermon is necessary. Scripture and song tell the complete story of redemption. Both services, at least for me, are two of the most powerful of the year.

The Easter Vigil is actually the first Easter service each year. It is the first service to declare the resurrection of Christ and the first in which we sing Easter's hallelujahs. The Easter Vigil begins outdoors (in our case, in an actual garden) in the darkness, emulating the darkness and grief of Holy Saturday. The congregation gathers around a small campfire where the Paschal candle (or Christ candle) is lit. The congregation then processes behind the person bearing the Christ candle, as we sing, "The light of Christ rises in glory, overcoming the darkness of sin and death."[1]

The procession slowly enters into the completely darkened chapel, signifying the darkness of Jesus's tomb on Holy Saturday evening. We symbolically enter the tomb of Jesus, where, for the next two hours, illuminated only by the light of the Paschal candle, we will remember through Scripture and hymns the creation and salvation history of the children of God. If you're not familiar with the Easter Vigil, it is much like Lessons and Carols for Easter.

The first reading from Genesis 1 tells of God creating the world, calling forth light, giving order to the waters and land and to night and day, of God speaking plants, then creatures of the earth, sea, and sky into being: "And God saw that it was good"

(Genesis 1:25). "So God created humans in his image, in the image of God he created them; male and female he created them.... God saw everything that he had made, and indeed, it was very good" (Genesis 1:27, 31).

As we all know, things don't remain good for very long. Chapters 2 through 11 of Genesis remind us of how humanity seems determined not to live into the image of its Creator, but to spiral back into the primordial chaos that existed before Creation. And that's the whole point of Lent. Things often do not go swimmingly in our lives or in the world. Sometimes that is due to our own actions, inaction, or the actions of those around us. However, the good news of Easter, as reflected in the Easter Vigil, is that God continuously seeks ways to redeem those whom God has created, to bring them out of their self-induced chaos and back into a rightfully ordered relationship with the One who breathed into them the sacred breath of life—to remind them (us included) of the One whose image they bear.

What struck me as I was leading my first Easter Vigil is that the next three readings in the service depict ways in which God attempts to redeem and restore all of creation and humanity. God does this through covenants God makes, first with all of creation (through Noah), then with Abraham, and then with the people of Israel through Moses.[2] Actually, many of the Scripture readings during the Lenten season lift up, or hint at, these covenants. Understanding God's covenants is basic and vital to a deeper understanding of Jesus's journey to the cross and his resurrection, and to our understanding of God's deep, abiding love and faithfulness to creation and all of God's children—even in the midst of our faithlessness.

So, What Is a Covenant?

Beginning in Genesis, God enters into one covenant after another with various humans in order to redeem and save God's creation. So, what is a covenant—and why would God choose to reach out to humanity through covenants as a way to prove God's sincerity and faithfulness in providing what's best for God's children and all of creation?

Covenant is one of the major theological motifs of the Hebrew and Christian Scriptures. Eventually, the terms "old covenant" and "new covenant," which once described two eras (Jeremiah 31:31-33; 2 Corinthians 3:4-11), came to refer to the two parts of the Christian Bible, the Old Testament (Covenant) and the New. But as the Scriptures employed in the Easter Vigil suggest, there really is one unbroken story—one covenant of love that God continuously reaffirms in response to human failing and faithlessness.

The Hebrew word for covenant, *berit,* means "bond," or "fetter," bringing to mind the binding or bonding of a relationship. In Greek, the language of the New Testament, the word for covenant is *diatheke*, which is also used for "will" or "testament." We might be tempted to think of a covenant much like today's contracts, in the sense that a contract provides protection or coverage as we try to meet someone halfway in a legal transaction. However, a covenant was always considered much more than a legal contract.

This, of course, is why, when I am officiating a wedding, I remind couples that they are entering not into a contractual fifty-fifty agreement but a covenant relationship. That covenant is one in which God is also a party. God is present as a witness and also as one whose faithfulness, love, and presence will provide the couple with the love, wisdom, patience, and endurance they will need to thrive in their marriage and faithfully meet the obligations of the covenant made between them. During the wedding ceremony, as couples make their promises they are made to realize (or at least hear of) their obligations toward one another. The rite that seals the covenant is the wedding service, complete with vows (sacred oaths).

The signs of the covenant are exchanged in the form of rings. The wedding ring, as the ritual language indicates, "is the outward and visible sign of an inward and spiritual grace, signifying to all the uniting"[3] of this couple—or the "binding" of this couple. The sign of the covenant, the wedding ring, tells everyone that these two persons have entered into a covenant relationship with one another before God. Prayers of blessing follow, along with a celebratory meal. All of this is indicative of the kind of covenant relationship God enters into with people throughout biblical history.

Secular covenants between persons are also mentioned in the Bible. There are covenants between two leaders (Abraham and Abimelech, Genesis 21:25-32); between heads of state (Ahab and Ben-hadad, 1 Kings 20:34); between a king and his people (David and the elders of Israel, 1 Chronicles 11:3); and between a conquering king and his vassal (Nebuchadnezzar and a Judean prince, Ezekiel 17:13-19; 1 Samuel 11:1). These covenants, or treaties, were thought to have been overseen by God. This was presumed to have been the case, for example, in the covenant made between Laban and his son-in-law, Jacob. The covenant concluded with a sacred meal where prayers were offered that God would make certain both parties kept the terms of the covenant (Genesis 31:44-54). David and his dear friend Jonathan also made a covenant of loyalty to one another "before Yahweh" (1 Samuel 23:18).

You can see how covenants were an integral part of the ancient Near East. They express an important element in the religious life of those living in ancient Israel. Israel saw itself as bound to one God, who, faithfully and lovingly laid claim to their lives and their loyalty.

Just as there were different types of covenants executed in the secular world of the ancient Near East, so, too, God institutes different kinds of covenants with God's people. Some are unilateral, meaning that only God has an obligation to the people of God or to creation. Other covenants require fidelity and obligations from both parties (much like the marriage covenant).

In what follows, we will explore each of the four major covenants in the Old Testament and see how they impacted the people who entered into those covenants with God, how God remembered each of them, and how each covenant relates to Jesus's journey to the cross. We also will explore how they impact our own lives and the world today in light of Easter and the Resurrection.

> ### It has eternally been God's nature to create and to save.

It has eternally been God's nature to create and to save. Out of God's love for creation, God is always seeking to redeem and make new. Covenants, an integral part of God's acts in creating, and saving, illustrate how God loves us, remembers us, and calls us to remember too. The bedrock of our salvation history includes those covenants made by God through Noah, Abraham, Moses, and David. These covenants provide a rich biblical understanding of, and serve as signposts to, the "new covenant" (Luke 22:20) and "new commandment" (John 13:34) instituted by Jesus on the night he gave up his life for us. It is a covenant that reveals the infinite depth of God's love for us from the beginning and demonstrates God's desire to save and bring new life to all who are created in the image of God. This ultimate covenant's climactic revelation occurs at the cross.

Throughout biblical history, humanity consistently breaks covenant with God, and God inevitably responds by rescuing and redeeming. This begins with Adam and Eve. Although they had no formal covenant with God, Adam and Eve received instruction and an understanding of how their relationships were ordered: God provided everything they needed, and they trusted in God completely—until they didn't and broke trust with God by eating the one fruit that was forbidden. They had a harmonious relationship with God until they tried to become like God and usurp God's place in their lives.

> *Throughout biblical history, humanity consistently breaks covenant with God, and God inevitably responds by rescuing and redeeming.*

The story of Adam and Eve sets the tone and establishes the pattern for the succession of broken relationships between God and humans, continuing through the story of the people of Israel (whose very name means to struggle or wrestle with God). Their story is our story. In every instance of rebellion or faithlessness committed by the people, God remains faithful. Or as the Communion liturgy in our church tradition reads: "You formed us in your image and breathed into us the breath of life. When we turned away, and our love failed, your love remained steadfast."[4]

In a way, the cross represents the ultimate breach of the covenant—not just the rejection of Jesus, God in human form, but an attempt to banish God among us forever through physical execution. In spite of this brutal betrayal and rejection, God in Jesus the Christ never stops remembering those whom he loves. God remains faithful as always, loving us to the end. God returns to invite us back into a relationship of love and trust that has been extended to us since the beginning of time. This time, God offers the power of God's very presence through the Holy Spirit to enable us to remain bound in covenant relationship with God the Father, Son, and Holy Spirit.

The Easter Vigil begins in darkness, like the darkness of a tomb, and with stories of God's redeeming covenants. Those covenants are meant to show the world the deep grief God experiences over our insistence on living our lives in violence and chaos, and the depths God continually plumbs in order to save us from ourselves. But the Vigil ends in light, hope, and Resurrection glory. As the last Scripture, the gospel message declaring the good news of the Resurrection, is read, light is shared from the Paschal candle, passed from one person to the next (much like a Christmas Eve candlelight service), and the darkness of the tomb slowly recedes as each person receives the light of the resurrected Christ. Light fills the "tomb" as we all raise our candles high and sing our hallelujahs in unison to the great Easter hymn, "Christ the Lord Is Risen Today."

I'm excited that we are taking this Lenten journey together to explore the covenants God has made with all of us through Noah, Abraham, Moses, David, and Jesus. These covenants are integral to the arc of our salvation story from Creation through God's gracious acts in Jesus Christ. May your Lenten and Easter season be richer because of this journey from Creation to the cross. And may you experience the joy, hope, and light of the risen Christ as you remember the God who always remembers you.

CHAPTER ONE

Noah:

God's Covenant with Creation

Then God said to Noah and to his sons with him, "As for me, I am establishing my covenant with you and your descendants after you and with every living creature that is with you, the birds, the domestic animals, and every animal of the earth with you, as many as came out of the ark. I establish my covenant with you, that never again shall all flesh be cut off by the waters of a flood, and never again shall there be a flood to destroy the earth." God said, "This is the sign of the covenant that I make between me and you and every living creature that is with you, for all future generations: I have set my bow in the clouds, and it shall be a sign of the covenant between me and the earth. When I bring clouds over the earth and the bow is seen in the clouds, I will remember my covenant that is between me and you and every living creature of all flesh, and the waters shall never again become a flood to destroy all flesh. When the bow is in the clouds, I will see it and remember the everlasting covenant between God and every living creature of all flesh that is on the earth." God said to Noah, "This is the sign of the covenant that I have established between me and all flesh that is on the earth."

(Genesis 9:8-17)

I have spent my entire life as a resident of Texas, and I love it. In Texas, we often say, "If you don't like the weather in Texas, just wait a few minutes." Although that seems to be a common motto in other states as well, the truth is that the weather in Texas is relatively predictable—well, most of the time—at least in

1

the summers. It's almost a certainty that mid-May to at least mid-September will be hot, extremely hot, and that fall is just a cooler summer, with the changing colors and dropping of tree leaves occurring one day in November. That may be an exaggeration, but not by much.

However, winters in Texas can bring great variety in temperatures and weather patterns. On one December weekend, you might experience gorgeous, eighty-degree temperatures as you sit by the pool. The very next weekend, you could be walking in a winter wonderland and shoveling a bit of snow from your sidewalk. The truth about winter in Texas is that temperatures rarely dip below freezing, at least in my neck of the woods, and if they do, it's not by much, and it doesn't last long.

February 2021 was an exception. Just when we thought we had left the word "unprecedented" behind in 2020 with the COVID-19 crisis, the Great Texas Snowstorm arrived. As a friend of mine remarked, "I'm pretty tired of living in unprecedented times and events!" In some respects, we felt as if we were living in the unprecedented times of Noah during that week. Instead of rain falling for forty days and nights, it seemed as if the snow and ice would never stop, or that the freezing temperatures that dropped into the teens and single digits would never end. When the cold abated, the rains came, not pouring from clouds in the sky, but from millions of burst water pipes that froze when the Texas power grid failed and countless homes were left without heat (and then, of course, water). The indoor rains literally flooded thousands of homes and businesses. We all felt more than a little like Noah.

You are probably familiar with the story of Noah, if for no other reason than from days spent in children's Sunday school classes, or from seeing colorful images in children's rooms and books of animals being led two by two onto the ark.

In this biblical flood story, God basically "un-creates" the Eden-like world that God established in Creation in order to reestablish a new creation. But why?

In this biblical flood story, God basically "un-creates" the Eden-like world that God established in Creation in order to reestablish a new creation.

Prior to the story of Noah, we discover that humanity, which God created in God's own image and declared "good," had become corrupt. Scripture tells us that God "saw that the wickedness of humans was great in the earth," that it was filled with violence and corruption. There "was only evil continually. And the LORD was sorry that he had made humans on the earth, and it grieved him to his heart" (Genesis 6:5-6).

Notice that this Scripture doesn't say that God seeks vengeance or is wrathful in response to what has happened. God surveys what has become of God's beautiful creation and of those who were tenderly entrusted with its care and is grieved to the heart.

That grief began with the disobedience of Adam and Eve in the garden of Eden after they ate from the fruit of the tree of the knowledge of good and evil. The intimacy and trust that had been inherent from the beginning were broken. Humanity began hiding from God, and then blaming one another, and even God, for their own transgressions. While the creation of humanity and the instructions God offers them (the boundaries put in place for their good) is not called or considered a covenant, faith and trust are broken. It's grievous.

And that grief continues as the first child born to Adam and Eve, Cain, murders his brother Abel. Even so, God still provides for Adam and Eve and offers a means of protection for Cain in the midst of his banishment (Genesis 3:21; 4). As an aside, perhaps it's worth pausing for a moment to reflect that the first murderer does not receive a capital sentence from God; instead, God's mark warns other humans not to impose such a punishment. As creation multiplies, it seems the growth of civilization only contributes to it becoming less civilized. Its actions are more and more inclined toward evil.

God is devastated by grief as the image of the loving and gracious Creator becomes unrecognizable in the ones who have been created. So God decides to "undo" creation. But instead of putting an end to it all, God decides to preserve a remnant of what God had created and start anew with the only person God finds to be righteous and blameless, the only one that "walked with God" (Genesis 6:9): Noah and his family. To begin this undoing of creation God determines to send a torrent of rain, a flood that will wash away all of the evil from the world and make way for a renewed creation.

Sometimes the image of God in us seems less visible to others than it should. We wander away from God and become less patient, less kind, less giving, less forgiving, less loving. In that wandering, we sometimes become more demanding, more irritable, more selfish, and more judgmental. We need to be re-created. We need to have God wash away that which makes our true identity as a child of God unrecognizable. We need to die to that which does not look like the love of the Creator in us.

In the ancient Near East, turbulent water was the symbol of ultimate chaos. A flood was viewed as a return to the primordial chaos from which God created the world. What is surprising about the story of Noah is not that God grieved over humanity and decided to eradicate it, but that the very people who were called into being out of the chaos and nothingness in creation, and were imbued with the very breath of God, seem determined to return to chaos and nothingness.

This wasn't just the case in Noah's day. We only have to turn on the television news or open our news apps to see story upon story of violence, corruption, greed, moral degeneration, and environmental abuses to realize that we, too, often choose turbulence and primordial chaos over the Eden-like existence that

God desires for us. Our all-too-human behaviors bring about real self-inflicted consequences. Our overt insistence on blaming the other person, the other political party, the other social class, or the other religious group for all of our personal and societal problems has resulted in a stark increase in vitriol toward our neighbors.

Our refusal to listen to others' points of view leads us no longer to see them as our brothers and sisters in creation, as children of God with whom we share this small planet that our Creator made. Our refusal to curb our appetites for consuming fossil fuels and refrain from littering our planet has contributed to rising sea levels, which can eerily remind us of the rising waters in Noah's day—this time caused by humans. Selfishness and violence have, as in Noah's time, contributed to fearfulness and suspicion in our communities instead of empathy and sharing.

It is easy to see the story of Noah, as many people do, as the act of a vengeful or capricious God. But that is not what is happening here. It's important to note that many of the ancient Near Eastern cultures had a flood story. Obviously, there was a massive flood (or floods) that affected the region, but each culture had its own story of what caused the flood. The most famous is the Epic of Gilgamesh.

The God of Israel created and governed the world with a benevolent purpose.

All of the other stories, except for the Old Testament interpretation of this natural disaster, marked the event as the work of capricious and uncaring deities, who made erratic and arbitrary decisions regarding the fate of humanity. However, Israel grounded this story in the God who cared deeply for all of creation and had expectations for righteousness and justice as part of the created order. The God of Israel created and governed the world with a benevolent purpose.

There is ample evidence for the judgment and justice that God pronounces through the Flood story. But it also isn't surprising that God relents from destroying everyone and everything by saving righteous Noah and his family, and two of every animal, in order to begin creation again. While God is definitely just, Scripture constantly reminds us that God is also gracious, merciful, slow to anger, and abounding in steadfast love (Psalm 86:15; Exodus 34:6; Numbers 14:18; Nehemiah 9:17). It is in God's very nature to create. It is also in God's nature to save and seek reconciliation with those who wander from the intention of their original design and blessedness. So, instead of destroying all of creation, God reboots it.

Before the rains come, God offers detailed instructions as to how Noah and his sons should build an ark to house their families and all of the animals when the waters begin to rise (Genesis 6:14-16). Just as God created birds of the air and every creeping thing on the earth, God provides for their reestablishment on the earth after the Flood in these words to Noah:

> "For my part, I am going to bring a flood of waters on the earth, to destroy from under heaven all flesh in which is the breath of life; everything that is on the earth shall die. But I will establish my covenant with you; and you shall come into the ark, you, your sons, your wife, and your sons' wives with you. And of every living thing, of all flesh, you shall bring two of every kind into the ark, to keep them alive with you; they shall be male and female. . . . Also take with you every kind of food that is eaten, and store it up, and it shall serve as food for you and for them." Noah did this; he did all that God commanded him."
> (Genesis 6:17-19, 21-22)

Here we see the beginning of God establishing the first covenant in the Bible. While we don't yet read what it will entail, we do see that this covenant will be a divine response to the tension held between God's unrelenting purpose to create a peace-filled world and the Creator of the universe's character of justice, colliding with God's deep love and compassion for a humanity that insists on bending toward violence, destruction, disobedience, and insubordination.

The church in which I served in ministry for 20 years—it is still my home church—is beautifully constructed in Gothic style. The sanctuary, like many churches, is architecturally designed in a cruciform shape. Its ceiling soars in height, seemingly carrying those who gather for worship into the presence of God. In such churches the center aisle is called the *nave*. The word *nave* is derived from the Latin, *navis*, meaning "ship." I used to love reminding our congregation to look up at the ceiling in the nave of our church because it was intentionally designed to look like the hull of a ship. Every time we gather for worship we are symbolically reminded, not only of the story of Noah, but also of God's saving grace that continues to carry the community of faith—you and me—to safety through all of life's deluges, turbulent waters, and storms. We are to remember what God has done in the past, and continues doing, to save us, shelter us, and lead us to life. That beautiful symbolism was derived from and began with Noah, an ark, and a covenant. The symbol of the church is still a ship, an ark.

It's interesting to note that the only other place in the Old Testament where the Hebrew word for ark (*tebah*) is used is in the story of baby Moses, who is placed in a pitch-coated "basket" (*tebah*) that protects him and carries him to safety. Pharaoh had ordered all male Hebrew babies to be thrown in the Nile and drowned. But this tiny ark carried Moses safely through the same water meant for his destruction. The same God that provides an ark for Noah and his family provides one for Moses, too.

After forty days of deluge, "God remembered Noah" and all the animals with him. "And God made a wind blow over the earth" (Genesis 8:1). After 150 days of roiling water, and months of waiting for the waters to recede, a dove that Noah releases from the ark finally returns with an olive branch signaling that it's time for the occupants of the ark to make their way into an empty world filled with new, hope-filled possibilities (Genesis 8:10-12).

God remembering Noah marks the turning point in the story. We learn here that God's memory is salvific, offering deeds of love that fulfill God's promises. For Noah, that promise is that he and his family will be integral in participating in God's new creation.

God's salvific remembering continues throughout the Bible. God remembers the childless Rachel, and she conceives and gives birth to Joseph (30:22-24). God hears the cries of the Israelites in Egypt, remembers the covenant made with Abraham, and delivers them from slavery (Exodus 2:23-25). The thief on the cross next to Jesus cries out to him, "Remember me when you come in your kingdom" (Luke 23:42). This was more than a throw-away request from a criminal; it was a declaration of faith in Jesus's identity as the One who can save through remembering the distress of God's people.

God remembers Noah and makes a wind blow over the earth, inviting us to remember the opening verses of the Creation story in Genesis: "When God began to create the heavens and the earth, the earth was complete chaos, and darkness covered the face of the deep, while a wind from God swept over the face of the waters" (Genesis 1:1-2).

In Hebrew the word translated as "wind" is *ruach*. It can also mean "breath" or "spirit." In creation, God's breath or spirit hovered over the waters of creation. That same breath and spirit breathe life into a lump of clay, causing it to become a human being made in the image of its Creator. That same wind, breath, and spirit will be active in this new creation, calming the waters and bringing new life. Keep all this in mind, by the way, whenever you read the story in John's Gospel of how the risen Jesus breathed onto the disciples and said to them, "Receive the Holy Spirit" (John 20:22). God's Spirit gave life to Adam and Eve, gave new life and power to the disciples, and, here, renews the world God made.

As the wind from God dries the earth, and as Noah and his family wait and yearn for new possibilities, we get a sense that God's grief continues. God realizes that retribution will not resolve humanity's constant bent toward chaos and destruction, so God makes binding promises to Noah and his family. This covenant actually extends to all humanity, all living creatures, and all creation.

As we've learned, some covenants require both parties to make an agreement, and if the covenant terms are not met, the covenant becomes void. What is amazing about this covenant that God makes with all of creation—with Noah, with you, and with me—is that it requires *nothing* from us. It is unilateral. God is the sole actor in this covenant made with creation. It sets limits only on God, who promises never again to destroy all of creation by a flood.

God self-imposes limits on God's power. And God places the rainbow in the sky as a kind of divine memory aid. Nothing is required of Noah and his family or of their descendants to prevent this destruction from recurring. Only God is responsible for keeping this covenant, and the sign of the covenant (if there's a covenant, there is usually a sign) will be the rainbow. Whenever it appears in the clouds, the rainbow will remind God of the covenant made with Noah and all of creation. Not that God has a poor memory and needs the reminder, but knowing about the sign of the covenant also reminds us that God prefers to bind God's self to us, regardless of how chaotic, violent, or destructive we become, rather than not live with us. It reminds us of our undeserved blessings and God's abundant compassion.

Just as God expresses sorrow in creating humanity and decides to begin creation anew, I believe God's initiating of the covenant with Noah expresses God's grief over the original creation that God loved. Why? Because God promises never again to do such a thing. Many have thought that the covenant given to Noah was a sign of God's repentance, or turning back toward humanity, even as God knows that this new creation, beginning with Noah's children and extending through their descendants, will not be as faithful and righteous as Noah. God would rather live with us, despite our disregard for God's purposes in our lives, than live without us. We can remember this and give thanks every time we see a rainbow.

One summer afternoon, as we were vacationing in Colorado, storms blew in over the Rockies, as they often do at that time of day. Just as the rain subsided, a magnificent rainbow appeared in the sky. It was the largest I had ever seen, with the most vibrant colors. It was so huge that it seemed as if you could almost reach out and touch it. The expansive bands were broad and as vivid as if a painter had freshly dipped his largest brush into each vibrant color on his palette. I grabbed my camera to capture the breathtaking moment. Though the images from the photos were impressive, they paled in comparison to the splendor of the reality.

And then I thought about Noah. I thought about how breathtaking it must have been for him to hear God's voice proclaim the depth of God's love for him, his family, and all of creation. I thought about how powerful and palpable that love must have felt. No doubt, the magnificence of the moment when Noah saw the first rainbow after God proclaimed the covenant with all of creation must have mirrored, or even amplified, the awe he felt at hearing about the covenant from God.

> **The rainbow was, and is, always there as a reminder that God remembers.**

And yet, even the story of the covenant, as it was told and read through the years, couldn't capture the magnificence of that first moment of awe, just as my camera couldn't capture the full beauty of my rainbow sighting or instill the wonder I experienced from witnessing it directly. People's memories faded like images in old photographs until humanity turned their eyes, not toward the rainbow in the sky, toward the sign of the everlasting covenant, but inward toward themselves and their desires. They began to forget. Yet the rainbow was, and is, always there as a reminder that God remembers.

An archer's "bow" was an instrument of war. An undrawn bow reminds us that God's "bow" is hung in the sky as a personal reminder to "never again" destroy the creation. By the same token, the rainbow, that undrawn bow in the clouds, helps us remember the God who remembers us—even, or especially, amid the chaos and rebellion we create. In delving into this story during the first week of Lent, we also begin our journey with Jesus toward Jerusalem and the cross.

Through Noah's story we can better understand not only the love and compassion of the Word made flesh who dwelt among us in Jesus but especially the God who sent him. We can better know the God who became one of us in order yet again to make us see that we are remembered as God's good creation, and not for our transgressions, our horrible tempers, our insistence on our own way, our violence, our vitriol, and our words. We are redeemed and offered to be re-created, over and over again. We are reminded of the deep, eternal love of our Creator, who will never stop seeking to be reconciled with us and who will suffer death on a cross in proving his love for us. In Jesus we are given a magnificent, vivid, unfading image of the God who remembers us.

Our salvation history is really a story of God being faithful to this covenant with humankind. Despite everything we do, God continues to reach out in new ways to preserve and restore the original relationship with humanity. In the story we see God reminding us of this steadfastness. This is evident in God's reassuring words offered to the Israelites through the prophet Isaiah as they were returning from exile in Babylon:

> I hid my face from you,
> but with everlasting love I will have compassion on you,

> says the LORD, your Redeemer.
> This is like the days of Noah to me:
> 　　Just as I swore that the waters of Noah
> 　　would never again go over the earth,
> so I have sworn that I will not be angry with you
> 　　and will not rebuke you.
> For the mountains may depart
> 　　and the hills may be removed,
> but my steadfast love shall not depart from you,
> 　　and my covenant of peace shall not be removed,
> 　　says the LORD, who has compassion on you.
> 　　　　　　　　　　　　　(Isaiah 54:8b-10)

This is the promise we see fulfilled, yet again, on the cross. In a way, the cross becomes our rainbow. The symbol of Jesus hanging on the cross, as represented in the Catholic tradition, reminds us of the steadfastness of God's love, which was willing to endure for our sake even the agony and torture of a public execution. The symbol of the empty cross, as represented in the Protestant tradition, reminds us that the cross is not the end—that it is actually a defeat for hate and violence and a victory for love that will outlast even the mountains and the hills. Like the rainbow, the sign of the cross is God's promise to us.

Remembering is important. It's important for us to remember the covenants God makes with us. It is also important to remember the covenants we make and the signs of those covenants. For those of you who are married, if you wear a wedding ring, as mentioned above, it is a sign of the covenant you made with your spouse, in the presence of God, as a witness to that covenant to love and be faithful to one another. It serves as a constant reminder of how couples are to live out their lives toward one another. Seeing that ring on our finger should be a reminder of our vows of fidelity to the ones we love.

When we receive Communion, we remember in the cup that this is the sign of Jesus's blood poured out for us for the forgiveness of sins. We remember his covenant to end our slavery to sin and death, to continue God's mission to create a peaceful world.

Our baptism, of course, is a sign of our entering that covenant. We are a new creation in Christ. The apostle Peter tells us that God's act of saving Noah and his family through the Flood was a precursor to our own baptism and the memory of our deliverance and salvation (1 Peter 3:18-22).

It is important to remember. Salvation is linked to remembering throughout the Bible.

What does this mean for us during Lent? Lent begins with Ash Wednesday. On Ash Wednesday we remember our mortality as we hear the words, "Remember that you are dust, and to dust you shall return."[1] These last few years, it seems to me, have been a constant reminder of our mortality. Deaths of ones we loved or knew well abounded because of COVID-19. Health workers succumbed to the disease or the stress of working so close to so much death. We see the horrific skyrocketing deaths due to rampant gun violence, the war in Ukraine, and natural disasters. We are constantly reminded of our mortality. We've had ample opportunity to reflect on the brevity of our days. But Lent is more than that.

> *Lent is a time to look inside to see how we might better spend our days on this earth in light of who and whose we are.*

Lent is also a call to spend forty days in the wilderness with Jesus as he overcomes the temptations we all face—the temptations to choose chaos over God—and begins his journey to the cross. Lent is a time to look inside to see how we might better spend our days on this earth in light of who and whose we are. It's a time for us to return to the One who remembers us so that we can live into the image of the One who created us. We are called to remember the cost of the covenants God makes on our behalf.

God's willingness to self-limit God's power and to sacrifice divine freedom in the story of Noah comes to a climax in the life, death, and resurrection of Jesus, who consummates God's relationship with us by embracing all of our life experiences, even death.

In Lent, we often commit to giving up things as a way of remembering Christ's sacrifice for us. I saw a meme in the week after the Great Texas Snowstorm that said, "Texans have Lent covered: We've given up heat, showers, and groceries. We do things big in Texas!" The beginning of Lent looked very different for our community that year. Instead of imposing ashes on Ash Wednesday, we prepared to open the church as a warming station, gathering funds, water, blankets, and food for those stranded without power or a roof over their heads.

The symbol of that week and that grace, for me anyway, was found in the water valve turn-off key. It's a large, heavy key, shaped like an anchor (at least in our neighborhood) that must be used to turn off water access to homes, usually in an alleyway. As pipes began to burst and homes in our neighborhoods began to flood, neighbors frantically raced to other neighbors' doors to see if they had that all-important key to save their homes from ruin. The anchor-shaped key seemed ironically appropriate in the midst of our indoor floods, and everyone wanted one of those anchors.

While many of us had been guarding our front doors during the pandemic as if they were bank vaults, in our neighborhoods that week we discovered that those doors were flung open wide for people who needed those keys, showers, or to come in from out of the cold for a few hours. People took on others' burdens by giving up blankets, diapers, infant formula, and water to help those displaced because of the storms. Some provided transportation to our homeless neighbors to get them to shelter. Neighbors showed up on each other's doorsteps wielding chainsaws to help clear fallen trees that had toppled from the weight of heavy ice.

And I thought, maybe this is the way Lent *should* look. Instead of just giving up something like candy for Lent, perhaps we would do well to reach out in concern to our neighbors who are suffering. Perhaps we could give up something we have an abundance of that someone else needs. Perhaps we could give up a few minutes or hours of our time to make a difference in someone else's life. Or as Pope Francis recommends, perhaps we could give up things like fear, impatience, resentment, gossip, negativity, and worry, to name a few.[2]

Lent calls us to journey with God and one another in a new way. A way that brings order out of the chaos in the world. If we "give up" something for Lent, the things we sacrifice should make a difference in the world. This does not necessarily mean giving up something beneficial to us. It means following Jesus toward a more profound richness in our lives and in the lives of those we touch. It means following in trust the way that Noah did. It means trusting the way that Adam and Eve did originally. It means trusting in the way Jesus encourages us to do when he invites us to consider the lilies of the field: "They neither toil nor spin, yet I tell you, even Solomon in all his glory was not clothed like one of these. But if God so clothes the grass of the field, which is alive today and tomorrow is thrown into the oven, will he not much more clothe you?" (Matthew 6:28b-30).

What if, instead of giving up chocolate, we decided to give up bitterness and anger or hurting others with our words or actions for forty days? What if we chose not to post derogatory posts on our social media pages? What if we made it a point to reach out to someone who is feeling deluged by darkness and storms in their life? What if we replaced bitterness, anger, political vitriol, pessimism, and hurtful words with kindness, gratitude, patience, and reconciliation? What if we remembered those whom God remembers but most of our society seems to forget?

In Judaism there is a concept known as *tikkun olam* that refers to the repair or healing of the world. In the Jewish understanding, when we reach out to those who are ignored or on the margins; when we comfort those who are hurting; when we lift up those who have fallen; when we bring healing to the sick and food to the hungry; we honor God's sovereignty by working to restore the beauty and harmony of God's creation. In our response to a broken world, like the world God saw in the time of Noah, we reaffirm God's commitment to create anew.

As we journey through Lent, may we remember the One who remembers us through the covenant of steadfast love. May the image of the rainbow in the sky prompt us to remember that the covenant applies not just to us as individuals but extends to all of our fellow children of God, created, like us, in the image of our Creator, and to creation itself. Through remembering, may we join in the self-limiting spirit of God's covenant, setting aside our own power and our own selfish desires, giving up who we have been for who we are yet to become—a renewed creation.

CHAPTER TWO

Abraham:
A Promise of Nations

When Abram was ninety-nine years old, the LORD appeared to Abram and said to him, "I am God Almighty; walk before me, and be blameless. And I will make my covenant between me and you and will make you exceedingly numerous." Then Abram fell on his face, and God said to him, "As for me, this is my covenant with you: You shall be the ancestor of a multitude of nations. No longer shall your name be Abram, but your name shall be Abraham, for I have made you the ancestor of a multitude of nations. I will make you exceedingly fruitful, and I will make nations of you, and kings shall come from you. I will establish my covenant between me and you and your offspring after you throughout their generations, for an everlasting covenant, to be God to you and to your offspring after you. And I will give to you and to your offspring after you the land where you are now an alien, all the land of Canaan, for a perpetual holding, and I will be their God." . . .

God said to Abraham, "As for Sarai your wife, you shall not call her Sarai, but Sarah shall be her name. I will bless her and also give you a son by her. I will bless her, and she shall give rise to nations; kings of peoples shall come from her."

(Genesis 17:1-8, 15-16)

The one righteous person God could find on earth, Noah, and his family were rescued from the primordial chaos of the Flood waters in order to begin creation again. This time, God hoped, humanity would live into its intended purpose, as those created in the image of the Creator. God makes a covenant with Noah, and all of creation, that God will never again destroy creation, offering the rainbow as a reminder of the covenant. In making that promise, it's as if God knows and understands that we will not be willing or able to fulfill God's hopes. God's heart will continue to be grieved by our chaotic actions and pleased in our moments of goodness. But the rainbow invites us to remember that God is not done with human beings.

The first eleven chapters of Genesis tell of God's all-encompassing love of creation, and of humanity's bent toward chaos, violence, self-centeredness, and evil. Beginning with Adam and Eve, humanity exerted its desire to want to be like God—to want to be their own god. This continues, of course, even after the time of Noah, but God is determined to maintain relationship with—to stay bound to—creatures who have both delighted and brought grief to God's heart, who like us, consistently turn away from God's grace. So instead of punishing errant humanity by flood or other means, God decides to see how things will work out if blessing is used as an alternative.

Despite the hope and promise offered by the rainbow, God's children continue to live according to their own desires, so God chooses one person through whom God will enact God's purposes for the world. God won't destroy all of creation in order to accomplish this mission. Instead, after developing a relationship with this one man, God will make another covenant, one that is narrower and more focused. Genesis 1–11 offers us a panoramic view of all of God's creation and the actions of all of humanity. In chapter 12 the focus narrows to one person and his family (like Noah, but we will see, also different), where things take a significant turn. Enter Abraham, or Abram, the name by which he has been known prior to his relationship with God.

God enters Abram's life at a time of great uncertainty. He is at a crossroads. His father and brother have died. He and his wife, Sarai, have taken their orphaned nephew, Lot, under their wing. Sarai has experienced infertility and now is long past childbearing age. In the midst of these great family challenges, God abruptly appears (as God often does), saying to Abram:

> "Go from your country and your kindred and your father's house to the land that I will show you. I will make of you a great nation, and I will bless you and make your name great, so that you will be a blessing. I will bless those who bless you, and the one who curses you I will curse, and in you all the families of the earth shall be blessed."

> So Abram went, as the LORD had told him, and Lot went with him. Abram was seventy-five years old when he departed from Haran.
> (Genesis 12:1-4)

God may have shifted the focus in what we call our salvation history, but these words, and the covenant to come with Abram, make clear that God's larger purpose has not changed. God is still intent on bringing human beings back into a relationship of complete faith and trust, a restoration of the Garden. With Abram, it's as if God goes back to the drawing board, inviting just one person into this circle of total trust that involves an unspecified "land I will show you" and a ridiculous-sounding, law-of-nature-defying promise of a child that will be born to an elderly couple.

If God's plan works, then the trusting relationship with Abram and Sarai will extend to this child of promise and to the child's children and the grandchildren's children. They will become a trusting family clan that will grow into extended networks of faithful tribes who will one day become a faithful nation. And through the faith of this nation, and the blessings it receives as faithful people living by choice under God's authority and purposes, the whole world will come, in the fullness of time, to recognize and revere the God of Abraham.

This family and the nation it becomes, through following the law of life God gives to them, is to be a light that reflects the character and nature of God to all of the nations of the world. In response to God's faithfulness to them, they are to live in such a way that everyone they encounter in their life's journey will be drawn closer to God and desire to live as they do—as those created in the Lord of Life's loving image.

> **Abraham's story is our story as well as Israel's story.**

This is why Abraham's story is our story as well as Israel's story. The roots of Christianity (and Judaism and Islam), the story of our faith heritage, grow out of Abraham's faith and the covenant God makes with him and his descendants. Abram may not have understood the eventual ramifications of God's promise, but we see, as the story of God's people unfolds, how the world would come to be blessed through him. We come to understand the appropriateness of both his original name, which means "exalted father," and the new name God gives him, which means "father of multitudes."

Why Abram?

If God's "Plan B" for the world depended on the faithfulness of one man, one couple, and one family, I can't help but ask myself, "Why?"

Doesn't it seem a little iffy, based on what we've seen up to this point in the Bible about God's experience with human beings, to have so much riding on a relationship with one person? And why this one? We know very little about Abram. We don't know anything about his character. We know nothing of his qualifications for which God is calling him. We don't know what his resumé looks like. God chooses Noah to begin creation again because Noah is righteous. Can the same be said of Abram? As of yet, we have no idea. It's tempting to wonder whether God considered others as well as Abram to go to some strange land that God would show them. Or was there something God saw in Abram and Sarai that led God to recognize them and their descendants as the sole choice with whom to begin a deeper relationship with human beings? We have no idea... or do we?

"So Abram went, as the Lord told him." Abram packs up his entire family and goes, literally, to God only knows where. He is told to leave his "country," his "kindred," and his "father's house"— basically everything he has ever known—to go to "the land that I will show you."

What I find astounding is that Abram doesn't argue with God and doesn't ask God any questions about where he is going. If you were being asked—or rather, told—to gather up your family and everything you owned and move to an undisclosed location, unless you were in the witness protection program, wouldn't you ask a few questions? I know I would.

As I began writing this chapter, I had just recently returned from a two-day speaking engagement. I had traveled only two hundred fifty miles from my home, but I planned meticulously for the trip. Before I left, I consulted the weather forecast in order to plan which outfits to wear. I packed an extra blouse, just in case I spilled coffee on one (which happens often). I packed shoes to match the outfits. I inquired of the church that hosted the event: At which hotel would I be staying? How close was it to the church? Would I need to bring technology for the slides that accompanied my presentation? Could they print copies of my notes, or would I need to bring copies with me? I logged the trip into my GPS to estimate how long the drive would take. All of that consulting, inquiring, and planning occurred for one quick little trip.

And yet, seventy-five-year-old Abram poses not one question. He just "went as the Lord told him." God calls, and Abram responds faithfully. So perhaps God chose Abram because God knew Abram's character, that he would faithfully follow where God led. Or perhaps Abram so desperately wanted God's promise to be true that, even though he was old and materially prosperous and set in his ways, he was willing to get up and go. After all, what God promises is amazing. It's not every day that a divine being promises to make an elderly, childless couple into a great nation whose descendants will be as numerous as the stars in the sky. It doesn't sound like a con, because con artists (like those who peddle promises on the internet that sound too good to be true) always require their victims to make some kind of financial investment or obligation. The only "ask" of Abram is to believe and to go.

The writer of Hebrews surmises that Abram took the first uncertain step of that journey in faith because he believed the Maker of Promises to be faithful in keeping promises (Hebrews 11:8-12). On behalf of himself and his yet unborn descendants, Abram says "yes" to becoming, like Noah, a new creation. What we will see is that one of the blessings the God of all creation will give to Abram and Sarai is to alter their inability to have children into the ability to "be fruitful and multiply" as directed in Genesis 1. They will be able to co-create the future with God through God's blessing.

By the Oak at Moreh

As Abram, Sarai, Lot, and their entire party (which would have included household servants, livestock, and all of their belongings) step out in faith, God leads them in the direction of Canaan. As they travel through this vast and rugged terrain, with no GPS except for God's leading, Abram and his entourage head south and take a pause in their journey in Shechem. There, in response to

Abram's faithfulness, God reinforces the promises declared earlier to Abram, painting them with additional color and texture.

As the group of road-weary travelers takes a break from their arduous journey, Abram stands under the shade of the Oak of Moreh. His eyes sweep across the glorious vista of the mountains before him, and his solitude is interrupted by the sound of God's voice: "To your offspring I will give this land" (Genesis 12:7).

In a sense, Abram has arrived: God shifts from leading him *toward* a new land to showing and promising that *this* land, as far as his eyes can see, will one day belong to Abram's offspring! This man who is childless at age seventy-five, whose wife is barren, will have children whose children will one day not just be nomads wandering through the land of Canaan, but will possess it!

> ## We can trust the Promise Maker
> ## to be the Promise Keeper.

While it must have been difficult for Abram and Sarai to leave everything behind, along the way God brings visual good news: There is a new promise that they can see with their own eyes. A promise for generations to come. Answering God's call opens up a new and promising future for them, and it does for us too. We can trust the Promise Maker to be the Promise Keeper.

Doubt, Reassurance, and the Beginning of a New Covenant

We have friends who own a ranch in Central Texas. We learned early on that when we're invited to travel there, *never* to drive a sedan but to take a large SUV. Why? Because once we turn off the main highway that leads to their home, the road is gravel, and maintenance on the road is unpredictable. It can be just a little bumpy, or there can be deep ruts, places that have been washed out from rains. Then there's the creek you must ford to continue on the gravel road. The creek could be dry, or it could be somewhat deep. You just never know. But in order to see our friends and enjoy their company, we have to make the bumpy, and sometimes deep crossing.

Sometimes, even when we're answering God's call, the journey can be difficult and the path doesn't seem clear, like traveling on a treacherous, bumpy, rocky passage with an occasional water hazard. We have doubts, reservations and disappointments, and then something reminds us why we should continue pursuing the journey on which we have been called. While we can't see what lies ahead, we're reminded God is faithful and can be trusted.

When I answered God's call to go to seminary, the first year was thrilling and exciting, and the long hours of study, reading, and writing seemed just fine. But by year two, my initial enthusiasm began to wane. My children (and probably my husband, too) were tired of eating macaroni and cheese and fast food. The rigorous workload, combined with the daily demands of being a mom, wife, and church employee, took a toll. I was exhausted, irritable, and stressed. I began to wonder whether I had made a mistake in going back to school. The incredible support of my husband was one of the few things that kept me encouraged to continue. (Among other things, he never complained about the food.)

One frustrating day, walking from the divinity school through the small forest that separates Southern Methodist University from the campus of Highland Park United Methodist Church, where my family attended and I served, I verbally chastised myself: "Why do you keep doing this to yourself?! Why don't you just quit?!" Immediately, those questions were answered as from my own mouth came the words, "Oh yeah, because God called me here." It was both a sobering moment as well as one of encouragement and recommitment.

Abram has such a moment (actually more than one, as we'll note later). He's been living a nomadic existence for what seems like forever. He is exhausted, stressed, and wondering if he might not be near the end of his life with no child to show for all of his faithful following. He wonders if he has made a mistake—or, worse, if God has made one. He fears that his only heir will not be a child of his own, but his servant, Eliezer (Genesis 15:2).

Just as God appeared, encouraging me to not give up on my call, God also appears to Abram offering these words of encouragement: "Do not be afraid, Abram, I am your shield; your reward shall be very great" (Genesis 15:1). God opens the conversation with a promise. God is Abram's shield, and he will have a great reward. On the surface, this is a promise of spoils for a battle Abram has just fought. But Abram counters God's promise with a question, "O Lord God, what will you give me, for I continue childless, and the heir of my house is Eliezer of Damascus?...You have given me no offspring, and so a slave born in my house is to be my heir" (Genesis 15:2-3).

In essence, Abram says to God, "What good are any spoils of war or reward to me if I can't pass them down to children? I've been doing what you asked all these years, and still have nothing to show for it. Why do I keep doing this to myself? Why don't I just quit?"

God calms Abram's frustrations with an encouraging promise, one that elicits Abram's recommitment to continue his journey with God. Essentially God says, "Abram, not only will you have a child that is biologically yours, but look up! Can you see the countless number of stars above your head? That is how numerous your descendants will be!" (Genesis 15:4-5, paraphrase mine). Next comes Abram's response: "And he believed the LORD; and the LORD reckoned it to him as righteousness" (Genesis 15:6).

Did you notice what happened here? Abram expresses doubt about God's promise, and God answers by reiterating the promise.

Why would Abram believe it? He's been through an enormous amount of trouble, and he still has no heir, and no pregnant wife. Earlier in Genesis we learn that Abram has been displaced by famine and driven further south into Egypt. There, he and Sarai experience a life-threatening altercation with Pharaoh (Genesis 12:10-20). When they return from Canaan, Lot is kidnapped by an enemy tribe. Abram and his servants come to Lot's aid by rushing into battle to rescue Lot (Genesis 14:1-16). Why should Abram believe God now? Because Abram remembers what God has done for him thus far. Abram sees God at work in leading him and Sarai into Egypt to save them from famine. Because of God's gracious care for them, they exit Egypt unharmed by Pharaoh and wealthier than when they arrived. Abram is grateful for Lot's rescue (Genesis 14:20). He knows he has already been blessed by God. He knows he can believe the promises of the Maker of Promises. And God counts his belief as righteousness. Abram, like Noah, may not be perfect, but he *is* righteous.

God can be trusted to keep God's promises.

As Abram's fears are calmed, he remembers the myriad ways he has experienced God's faithfulness in the past. Although Abram has yet to realize the fullness of God's promises, he continuously encounters the faithfulness of God. God can be trusted to keep God's promises.

I love this point in Abraham's story because it accentuates his humanity. Abram is susceptible to insecurities, doubts, and impatience, just like us. His story, especially in this season of Lent, reminds us that even you and I, with all of our foibles, can still be an exemplary model of faith. We, too, can be viewed by God as righteous.

The Lenten journey of self-reflection is one that requires time and patience. God's promise through Abram to us is that, if we remain committed to following God's lead, we have no need to doubt or fear, for God is trustworthy. God's leading will carry us into a future where we will still face difficulties, disappointments, and challenges, but it will also be a future brimming with purpose and fulfillment. One in which we are blessed to be a blessing.

Cutting a Covenant

A pattern began in Genesis 15:1-6 that we are about to see repeated in Genesis 15:7-19. God makes a promise, Abram questions, and God offers reassurance.

God reiterates the promise to give the land of Canaan to Abram by reminding him of who God is—the One who brought Abram from his homeland to Canaan. Then comes the question: "O Lord God, how am I to know that I shall possess it?" (15:8). The reassurance God gives Abram comes in the form of what seems very strange to us by twenty-first-century standards, and it begins with a rite instituted by God, a reassuring promise made by God to Abram through what is known as a theophany (God appearing as smoke or flame) and in making a covenant.

God instructs Abram to gather various animals and bring them to God. Abram then cuts all of the animals in two, laying the corresponding pieces across from each other so that there is a path between them. We might think that a sacrifice is about to take place, but it isn't a sacrifice. God is *making* a covenant (literally, "cutting," in Hebrew) with Abram. As the sun goes down and darkness descends, God tells Abram just how his descendants will come to possess the land. It will become a certainty, but only after spending four hundred years in slavery in an alien land; then they, like Abram did, will come out of that land (Egypt) with great possessions. He can die in peace knowing that this will all come to pass. But it will take patience on the part of Abram and his ancestors. To ensure that Abram believes him, God, in the symbolic form of smoke and fire, passes through the divided animal carcasses; it was a rite in the ancient Middle East in which participants invoked death upon themselves should they be unfaithful to the terms of the covenant. In essence, the covenant makers swear that they should become as the animals they are passing through if they are unfaithful to the covenant they have cut (see Jeremiah 34:18-20). God basically takes a blood oath, putting God's life on the line, in making this unilateral, promissory covenant with Abraham. God does not demand that Abram pass between the animals; God alone incurs the obligation. This entire rite becomes the answer to Abram's question. Abram's descendants will have *this* land, with spoils, as a home. As a matter of fact, it is not just a future gift, they are already living in the land they will one day possess.

God will never revoke this promise. While it is everlasting, it does not guarantee that every person in every generation has the privilege of participating in the fulfillment of the covenant.

God's salvation is worked out throughout this story and parallels other covenant stories. God chooses Noah, Abram, Moses, and David. God saves Noah from the Flood. God saves Abram (and later his descendants) from Egypt. God saves Moses from the waters of the Nile and his people from slavery under Pharaoh. God saves David from his enemies.

Ultimately, as we read throughout Lent, God chooses and sends God's own self, literally laying God's own life on the line for God's children in the form of Jesus, the Word made flesh.

A Detour and a Disruption

By this point in the story, it has been ten years since Abram and Sarai began their journey in search of becoming a "great nation." While Abram believes a child will be born to him as an heir, God never said anything specifically about Sarai. Naturally, they become impatient. Let's face it, they're not getting any younger! Instead of continuing to wait on God, they act on their own.

Sarai suggests that they use her slave, Hagar, as a surrogate so that they might have a child through her (Genesis 16:2). The child born to Hagar would legally belong to Sarai and Abram. What could possibly go wrong? According to Genesis...a *lot*.

Hagar becomes pregnant with a precious baby boy, who is named (by God) Ishmael, meaning "God listens." Predictably, a bitter rivalry erupts between Sarai and Hagar. Sarai cruelly mistreats Hagar, who is only viewed as property. Abram abets the behavior by doing nothing. Home life is miserable for everyone. But God is faithful to *everyone* involved. Abram becomes a father at eighty-six years of age (Genesis 16:9-16). While Ishmael is loved by Abram and by God, and viewed jealously by Sarai, God has more in store. God can take what has become dysfunctional and broken and turn it into blessings.

Abram and Sarai believe that God's promises at the beginning of their journey, which were ratified with the cutting of a covenant by God, will become manifest through Ishmael. But God has only provided a detour for them—or did they create their own detour through their impatience? The Scriptures don't tell us, but we know that God has a laughable surprise in store for Abram and Sarai and some name-changing promises as well.

Many of us have experienced game-changing moments in our lives, like having children, buying a house, or getting married. These situations introduce elements of change in an existing situation. While some of life's moments are game-changers, others are also "name-changers." This is what Abram and Sarai experience.

Abram and God have been in a long-term, committed relationship for twenty-four years, ever since God first approached the seventy-five-year-old Abram at his home in Haran. But that relationship is about to be elevated to yet another level. God is going to introduce a new element to an existing situation, changing Abram's life, and ours, in a significant way. Everyone involved is about to have a name change, Abram, Sarai, and even God. God then provides for a sign of the covenant.

God interrupts one more time, telling the ninety-nine-year-old Abram: "I Am God Almighty" (El Shaddai, a name used here for the first time in the Torah). "Walk before me and be blameless," meaning, live life in an exemplary fashion so that my love and character will be obvious to everyone you meet. Walk in the way of faithfulness, generosity, and love. "And I will make my covenant between me and you and will make you exceedingly numerous." At the sound of God's voice and those words, Abram falls on his face. Is there a more appropriate response than to bow before God when one is about to enter into a covenant with God? Abram doesn't think so.

God introduces elements making this game-changing reality a name-changing event. God promises Abram will become the father of a "multitude" of nations, and kings shall be born from his lineage. God promises, not some but *all* the land of Canaan will be given to Abram's offspring perpetually. "And I will be their God." Abram, "exalted father," rises from the altar of God's covenant, with a new name and new identity: Abraham, "father of multitudes," or "father of many nations." His descendants, bearing the sign of the covenant, circumcision, will be marked for God's purposes. They will be God's chosen people (Genesis 17:1-13).

Although circumcision was practiced by others in the world at that time, God employs it to identify this new family of faith and the everlasting covenant made between them. God will *always* be God to Abraham's offspring. They will *always* be loved, cared for, and pursued by their God. Although the blessings of the covenant are unconditional, as in marriage, they only present themselves through faithfulness. Even if they turn away from the covenant and its blessings, God will never turn away from them.

This news alone could keep Abraham bowing before God for the rest of his life, but God has more in store! Sarai is also included in the covenant, receiving her own new name, Sarah, which means "Princess." After twenty-four years of yearning for her own child, within the year, the old and barren "Princess," God promises, will give birth to nations and kings through a son of her own, Isaac. The covenant will be secured through Isaac, not Ishmael (although God makes equally grand promises to care for Ishmael as well; see Genesis 17:20).

Upon hearing this truly unbelievable news, Abraham *again* falls on his face. But this time he doubles over, not in awe, but in laughter (Genesis 17:17)! Coincidentally, Sarah, when she hears the news later that she is going to give birth to a son, also laughs (see Genesis 18:9-15). It is no coincidence that the son born to them will be named Isaac, which means "He laughs," for God is about to fill Abraham's and Sarah's home with an abundance of life, joy, and laughter.

This covenant between God and Abraham is a reflection of God's relationship with all of Israel, and through Israel to the church, and through the church to each one of us (Romans 4:22-25; Ephesians 2:8-9; Galatians 3:6-9).

Hundreds of years after Abraham's death, his family does become a nation. One of the "kings" God promises through Abraham's lineage is David, and from David's lineage, Jesus is born. The promises of God to Abraham as, the apostle Paul reminds us, were made to his offspring, which includes Jesus the Christ. Our inheritance in Christ comes through the covenant God made with Abraham through faith (Galatians 3:16-18).

If you were baptized into the Christian faith, you experienced a sign of the covenant, an outward and visible sign of an inward and spiritual grace signifying to all that you are included in God's covenant and family of faith named "Christian." Your baptism was a name-changer. In baptism you received the promise that the Creator of the Universe is, and always will be, your God. Your

God will never break covenant with you. If you were baptized as an infant, you probably "confirmed" the baptismal vows your parents took on your behalf during a confirmation ceremony when you became older. Your infant baptism was recognition that God's grace and love were present with you, surrounding you, before you were even aware of it. Just as Jesus began his ministry saying yes to his calling through baptism (Matthew 3:16-17), so we who are baptized into the Christian faith say yes to our calling and ministry as Christ's followers, to walk before him in a life of obedience, reflecting his love to others.

Lent is a time for us to recall, to remember, our baptism and the vows we affirmed. Through baptism we are initiated into Christ's church, given "new birth." We have become a new creation through water and the Spirit, and all of this "is God's gift offered without price."

I love these words from the prayer that is offered before a person is baptized in my tradition, for they remind us of God's everlasting promises of salvation that began in Creation, and were offered in the covenants through Noah, Abraham, Moses, and Jesus:

> *Eternal Father:*
> *When nothing existed but chaos,*
> > *you swept across the dark waters*
> > *and brought forth light.*
> *In the days of Noah*
> > *you saved those on the ark through water. . . .*
> *When you saw your people as slaves in Egypt,*
> *you led them to freedom through the sea.*
> *Their children you brought through the Jordan*
> > *to the land which you promised.*
>
> *In the fullness of time you sent Jesus. . . .*
> *He called his disciples*
> > *to share in the baptism of his death and resurrection*
> > *and to make disciples of all nations.*[1]

You are a beloved child of God, descendant of Noah and Abraham, heir to the covenant. You are blessed to be a blessing, to share the love of God that is available to every person. During this Lenten season, may you follow the One who can lead you "to the land that I will show you," for that following will lead you to a land of blessing and abundance.

Following Jesus to the Places He Will Show Us

Jesus's relationship with his disciples began with simple, open-ended invitations. After his baptism by John in the wilderness by the Dead Sea, he invited Andrew and Simon (Peter) to "come and see." Beside the Sea of Galilee, Jesus invited prospective disciples to "follow me." It is strikingly like God's call to Abraham: Follow me "to the land that I will show you."

When we consider the similarities between God's call to Abraham and Jesus's call to his disciples (and to us), we may come to appreciate how our entire history with God has centered on God's desire to invite us into a new land of more profound relationship. The invitation is driven by God's inexhaustible love for us—a covenantal love that will not let us go, and relentlessly, creatively seeks new ways to reach us no matter how many times we turn away from God's love or fail to keep faith. Through Jesus, the covenant made with Abraham (and with Noah, Moses, and David) is extended to us again and again. No wonder the Easter Vigil begins by reading the covenant and redemption stories of God!

Through Jesus, the covenant made with Abraham (and with Noah, Moses, and David) is extended to us again and again.

33

Jesus speaks to us much like God spoke to Abraham. Imagine Jesus speaking these words to you: "Follow me to the land that I will show you. You may not know where we're going much of the time, but I do. Trust me. Walk before me. Follow my ways. Learn about my love. Watch me. Do as I do, and I will give you a new identity, one that fits with whom I've created you to be, one that equips you to live into the calling to which I have called you. And I will prepare a home for you, a place where you can flourish and belong, a place where you can grow in me and I in you."

Where has Jesus called you to follow in the past? Where do you think he is calling you now? Jesus has called me to many places and things. That following has led to unimaginable places I would have never considered venturing on my own. The path has also led through dark places filled with challenges, difficulty, and grief. However, God, through Jesus Christ, has always been with me, just as God was always with Abraham, was always with God's people as they wandered in the desert, was always with David as he sought to lead his kingdom, and was always with Noah and his family. Jesus both walks alongside and goes ahead to prepare us for what comes next.

In Christ, we, like Abraham, are also promised a "land," a home where we can live, feel secure, grow, and flourish. While John's Gospel speaks of that land or home in a way that appears to be in the afterlife (John 14:2), it is true that any place where we walk with Jesus is home. Jesus goes before us to all of the rooms of our lives, prepares the way for us, and leads us there.

As the disciples learn along their journey, as we learn as Jesus's disciples, and as Lent reminds us, we are called to follow Jesus to the cross. It is a fearful place that represents the worst in human beings, a place that represents an assertion of human power over the power of God's love and light. We don't want to go there. Even Jesus asked if he might be spared the cross, if it might be God's will.

In the end, Jesus remained faithful to his call, and he calls us to be faithful too. If we follow Jesus to the cross, we discover that the worst is not the last. It is a way station along the journey that takes us to our promised land, an eternal home in the presence of God.

Near the end of our Christian Scriptures, the writer of Revelation, John the Evangelist, urges the struggling Christian communities of Asia Minor (western Turkey today) to continue to follow in spite of the difficulty of their journey, to remain faithful to their calling. He paints a vivid and beautiful picture of the place God has prepared—a new Jerusalem and a new earth (Revelation 21 and 22). There are no fortified walls around the city, because there are no longer enemies to fear. There are no gates to keep people out because everyone is welcome. There is no need for artificial light so people can find their way in the dark because everyone will walk by the light of God's glory. A river of life runs through the city, where there is no more suffering or human tears, and death is abolished forever. As in the garden where human beings first lived in God's presence, and knew God face-to-face, there is a fruit-bearing tree. But this tree is not forbidden. Its leaves, John tells us, are for the healing of the nations.

Unlike Abraham, and unlike the disciples at the time they accepted Jesus's invitation to follow, we know the ultimate place that God will show us. We have received glimpses of what it looks like. We can believe the promise because the living Jesus has shown us it is real. In rising from death, Jesus showed us where the journey ends. Because he lives, we can follow without fear. Jesus in effect says, "My cross has the power of freedom. Freedom from violence, destruction, injustice, and death. If you take up your cross and follow me, you will discover a love that is rich beyond comparison. You will come home, and be home, where you belong." In accepting God's reign over our lives and following the path Jesus has marked for us, we can overcome the world to experience the abundance of God's kingdom here and now. We can experience the forever of an intimate, trusting relationship with God that God always wanted to have with us, in a restored garden, a paradise.

As we journey through Lent together, my prayer is that you will remember the promise made and fulfilled through Abraham, and that the memory of this eternal covenant will help you have the faith to follow, without fear, to the cross and beyond, all the way home to God.

CHAPTER THREE

Moses and Israel:
Words of Life and Freedom

"You have seen what I did to the Egyptians and how I bore you on eagles' wings and brought you to myself. Now, therefore, if you obey my voice and keep my covenant, you shall be my treasured possession out of all the peoples. Indeed, the whole earth is mine, but you shall be for me a priestly kingdom and a holy nation."

(Exodus 19:4-6)

Then God spoke all these words:

"I am the LORD your God, who brought you out of the land of Egypt, out of the house of slavery; you shall have no other gods before me.

"You shall not make for yourself an idol, whether in the form of anything that is in heaven above or that is on the earth beneath. . . .

You shall not make wrongful use of the name of the LORD your God. . . .

Remember the Sabbath day and keep it holy."

(Exodus 20: 1-4, 7-8)

And thus begins God's words to the Israelites enslaved in Egypt, inviting them into a covenant of life-giving freedom, freedom they will experience if they intentionally live within the parameters set before them by their liberating God who treasures them.

Psychologists tell us that children need good boundaries in their lives. As counterintuitive as it may seem, especially to teenagers, they need enforced rules and limits to make them feel loved and secure. A friend of mine likens this to walking across a narrow bridge over an expanse of turbulent water. A bridge with guardrails gives you a greater sense of security than one without them. And, in a way, that security gives you freedom. It reduces the likelihood of losing your balance and falling off the narrow bridge. You're free to walk across that bridge without fear. You have something to hold on to as you make your way.

When they were young, our children had quite different opinions about the rules and boundaries we established. Our daughter loved having rules, knowing what the rules were, and the limits we had set for her. If she went to a friend's house to play or spend the night, and there seemed to be no clear rules, she would make up her own. They gave her a sense of security. On the other hand, our son liked testing boundaries from as early as we can remember. For instance, if we said very specifically:

"You can play outside, but you can't cross the street. You cannot step foot in the street. Do you understand the rules?"

"Yes, ma'am."

"Can you repeat them back to me, please?" (He would, word by word.)

Inevitably, I would look out the window to find him defiantly straddling the curb with one foot in our yard and one foot in the street! Really? Yes, really. I'm unsure if he wanted to break the rules because he didn't like them, he had a death wish, or if he was testing the rules to ensure they would hold—giving him a greater sense of security. And inevitably, he would end up in time-out with his play time, and the freedom we as parents longed to offer him, cut short. In their differing ways, both our son and daughter wanted to experience the same thing: a sense of security and knowing they were loved.

> *We need boundaries to keep us safe so we can thrive in our relationships with each other, the community around us, and God.*

As parents, we establish rules because we love our children. We want them to be safe, feel secure, and avoid unnecessary problems in life. We want them to thrive in their relationships with others and the world around them. Children need good boundaries. The same is true for all of us, whether we are five or ninety-five. We need boundaries to keep us safe so we can thrive in our relationships with each other, the community around us, and God.

God, the Perfect Parent

God, as the perfect divine parent, has set boundaries for us so that we may thrive in the way God intends. It is notable how often the relationship between God and humans is depicted in the Bible as that between a parent to their children. Scriptures often speak of God as both father and mother, beginning with Genesis, where we discover that we are created, both "male and female," *in the image of God* (Genesis 1:27). Deuteronomy 32:18 speaks of God in both masculine and feminine terms, as both a father and as a mother who gave us birth. We know that God is neither male nor female, for "God is spirit" (John 4:24). God transcends gender. Yet God exhibits anthropomorphic characteristics that can be identified as paternal and maternal so that we may fully and more intimately experience God's presence.

The most common parental reference to God in the Bible is that of a father. Here are a few examples:

> Yet, O LORD, you are our father;
>> we are the clay, and you our potter;
>> we are all the work of your hand.
>>> (Isaiah 64:8)

39

*See what love the Father has given us, that we should be called children
of God; and that is what we are.*

(1 John 3:1)

*I will live in them and walk among them,
    and I will be their God,
    and they shall be my people. . . .
and I will be your father,
    and you shall be my sons and daughters,
says the Lord Almighty.*

(2 Corinthians 6:16b, 18)[1]

There are also familiar images of God as a mother. The prophet
Isaiah is most fond of this imagery, as noted in these verses:

*As a mother comforts her child,
    so I [God] will comfort you.*

(Isaiah 66:13)

*Now I will cry out like a woman in labor,
    I will gasp and pant.*

(Isaiah 42:14b)

*Can a woman forget her nursing child,
    or show no compassion for the child of her womb?
Even these might forget,
    yet I will not forget you.
See, I have inscribed you on the palms of my hands.*

(Isaiah 49:15-16a)

Other common images of God seen in Deuteronomy 32:10-11,
Ruth 2:12, Psalm 17:8, and Psalm 57:1 (to name a few) are that
of a mothering bird protecting her chicks under her wings or that
of a mother eagle catching her chicks from falling to their death
as they learn to fly. Jesus himself utilizes this mother hen imagery
as he weeps over the city where he will be crucified: "Jerusalem,
Jerusalem, the city that kills the prophets and stones those who
are sent to it! How often have I desired to gather your children

together as a hen gathers her brood under her wings, and you were not willing!" (Matthew 23:37; Luke 13:34).

> **There is no doubt that God is our divine parent.**

These images portray God as protecting God's children, sheltering them as they grow in strength and independence. There is no doubt, as the Gospel of John tells us, that God is our divine parent: "To all who received him [Jesus], who believed in his name, he gave power to become children of God, who were born, not of blood or of the will of the flesh or of the will of man, but of God" (John 1:12-13).

Incorporating both images of God as mother and father is not some radically new idea. It is as old as, well, the Bible. And thankfully, our heavenly parent has provided us with wonderful boundaries within which to live—boundaries that exist as part of God's covenant with Israel.

Boundaries for a Treasured Possession

In the previous two chapters of this study, we've looked at the first two covenants in the Old Testament and their importance for our lives today and our Lenten journey. We discover in God's covenant with Noah—with all of creation—that God's children, who broke God's rules since the beginning of time, are so loved by God that never again will God destroy it by a flood. God will always remember the love God has for all of creation.

Through God's covenant with old and childless Abraham and Sarah, we discover that we, along with Abraham's descendants, are God's people set apart to be a blessing to all the nations—to draw the world toward the One in whose image we are all created. We learn that God brings new life into places that are as good as dead.

It is God's nature to create. And it is God's nature to save God's people when they step outside the boundaries God provides for living or when they become marginalized and oppressed by others.

If we scan the territory between Abraham, beginning in Genesis 12, and Moses in Exodus 20, we discover that Abraham's descendants, as promised, become as numerous as the grains of sand in the wilderness or stars in the night sky. They also become slaves in Egypt for four hundred years (as foretold by God to Abraham in Genesis 17). There is not enough space here to fully recall how Abraham's descendants flourished and then came to settle in Egypt, where they initially lived in peace and prosperity. I encourage you to read it for yourself in Genesis; it's an amazing and powerful narrative. However, in order to better understand the covenant God makes through Moses with the people who have come to be known as Israel, let's briefly recap the story.

After Abraham's grandson, Jacob (later renamed "Israel" by God), and his twelve sons and their families relocate to Egypt to escape a famine, the Israelites became quite prolific in the land of Egypt. Scripture tells us that the land was "filled with them" (Exodus 1:7). Generations passed, and a new ruler came to power in Egypt, one that had no recollection of Joseph (one of Israel's sons) and no regard for his special relationship with the earlier pharaoh. In this pharaoh's eyes, the enormous population of Israelites threatened Egypt's society and even their security.

So the Israelites were enslaved and oppressed by the hard labor of building projects instituted by Pharaoh. To add to their pain and suffering and to diminish their growing numbers, Pharaoh commands that the Hebrew midwives kill all Hebrew boys as soon as they are born. In an act of civil disobedience, two midwives insist that the vigorous Hebrew women are giving birth before the midwives can arrive. And so Pharaoh tries another tack, commanding that all Hebrew boys be thrown into the Nile and drowned (Exodus 1:19-22).

Moses and an Ark

This is where we pick up the story of Moses. God will enact another salvation story through an ark (*tebah*). This time, the ark is tiny, only large enough to hold one small male Hebrew baby. And that baby will be delivered alive from the waters of the Nile—waters intended by Pharaoh to be the infant's grave. Through the instruction and grace of God, that baby will deliver an entire nation from the death-inducing life of enslavement and oppression into life-giving freedom in the presence of God.

A young Levite woman secretly gives birth to a baby boy. Desperate to save his life, she hides him at home as long as she possibly can. After three months have passed, she takes a papyrus basket and covers it with bitumen and pitch to make it waterproof. Bitumen today is made from distilling crude oil but also occurs naturally in river bottoms. Its viscosity makes it perfect for paving roads or waterproofing a makeshift bassinet-turned-ark.

Lovingly and tenderly, the baby's mother places him into the ark and slips it among the reeds near the riverbank on the Nile. Scripture doesn't tell us this, but I imagine his mother praying for God to spare his life and deliver him to someone who would raise him in a loving home. The baby's sister follows closely to see what happens.

What happens is that Pharaoh's daughter comes down to the river at the very same time to take a bath. I suspect this was more than mere coincidence. The Hebrew woman probably knew the routine of Pharaoh's daughter and timed the launching of Moses's little ark so that it was likely to be found by the royal entourage. Perhaps she even reasoned that the baby's best chance of survival was to be discovered by Egyptian women with royal power and connections. If so, then events unfolded just as the Hebrew woman had hoped.

Pharaoh's daughter spies the little basket among the reeds and opens it. She realizes the crying baby is a Hebrew, marked for death, but she is so filled with compassion for him that she cannot do what her father commands. Instead, in an act of quiet rebellion, she decides to keep the baby and raise it as her own. The baby's sister, who conveniently happens to be standing nearby, offers to find a woman to nurse the child for Pharaoh's daughter. Well, you can guess who gets to keep caring for this baby lifted from the Nile. Pharaoh's daughter appropriately names the baby Moses (*Mosheh* in Hebrew), which means draw out (of the water), rescue, or deliver.

Moses is raised as an Egyptian by Pharaoh's daughter, but he knows who his people are—probably because his own mother and sister were involved in his upbringing. He sees their oppression. One day, out of his sense of justice, Moses strikes and murders an Egyptian who is mistreating one of the Hebrew slaves. When Pharaoh discovers what Moses has done, he seeks to kill him. Moses flees and begins a new life in the land of Midian. There, as he sits by a well one day, he meets the seven daughters of Reuel, the priest of Midian, and helps them water their sheep. Moses eventually marries one of the priest's daughters, Zipporah, and lives many years as a shepherd for Reuel, the priest (Exodus 2:11-22). Have you noticed how some of the great leaders of Israel begin their lives as shepherds? Moses and King David are prime examples.

More years pass. Out of their misery, the enslaved Israelites in Egypt cry out to God for help. "God heard their groaning, and God remembered his covenant with Abraham, Isaac, and Jacob" (Exodus 2:24). God *remembered* God's people. Salvation is coming.

Moses is minding his sheep one day on Mount Horeb, or Mount Sinai (as described in some versions of the Exodus story), when he sees a burning bush that is not being consumed by fire. Curious, he draws closer for a better look and encounters God. God calls out to him, "Moses, Moses!" and Moses answers, "Here I am" (Exodus 3:4). This is the same response many prophets offer when God calls them. Abraham, Isaiah, Jeremiah, and even Mary, the mother of Jesus, respond with these words when God or God's messenger calls their name. Moses is in good company.

The commanding voice emanating from the bush announces, "I am the God of your father, the God of Abraham, the God of Isaac, and the God of Jacob" (Exodus 3:6). Moses is awed by God's presence, but even more so when he hears what comes next. He has been chosen to go confront Pharaoh and lead God's people out of Egypt so they can worship God on this very mountain. The one who was drawn out of and delivered from the water will be the one to draw out and deliver God's people from slavery and into the land God has promised (Exodus 3:7-11).

Moses may have answered when God calls his name, but he is anything but eager to accept the call God places on him to go to Egypt and confront Pharaoh. He repeatedly tries to convince God to choose someone else. He presents one excuse after another. He is not important enough for the people, much less Pharaoh, to listen to him. He's not eloquent and is slow in speech. What if the Israelites want to know the name of the God who sent him? What if they don't believe his story about being sent by the God he encountered in the burning bush?

Don't we feel like Moses sometimes? Don't we, too, sense God calling us to a difficult task and ask, "Who am I to do this thing? I'm just a nobody. I'm not eloquent or persuasive. I'm not gifted in that way. Who am I to speak into the halls of power?" And God answers, "You may not be eloquent, persuasive, or gifted in a particular way. You may not be powerful. But I Am. I Am Who I Am. Tell the people 'I Am' has sent you. I will be with you, and that is enough for you. So go."

How different our lives would be, how different our communities would be if we lived as if we knew this was true. What if we took time during Lent to notice the burning bushes around us? What if we listened for the cries of our brothers and sisters who are laboring under what seems like generations of oppressive treatment? What if we truly believed that God could give us the right words when needed, or the confidence to speak up for those who can't speak for themselves?

So Moses goes, and I Am goes with him. They make a formidable team.

If you've seen Cecil B. DeMille's masterpiece, *The Ten Commandments*, we are at the place where Charlton Heston, portraying Moses, has brought the people through the plagues, the Passover, and the miraculous parting of the Red Sea. Now the entire company is back at the same place where Moses first met God: Mount Sinai.

As enslaved people, God's people haven't been able to make a decision for themselves in centuries. Now they are about to embark on a journey across the wilderness as God leads them to the Promised Land. But first, they need to understand a few things. They need to understand that God heard their cries in Egypt, saying, "I bore you [out of slavery] on eagles' wings and brought you to myself" (Exodus 19:4b). There are no more chains, no more backbreaking work seven days a week, no more being oppressed, no more answering to Pharaoh. Now God will make a covenant with them through Moses, speaking the words quoted at the beginning of this chapter and more.

Even before the Lord declares the terms of the covenant, all the people agree to it because they understand who has freed them! They now know they are the extension of God's covenant with Abraham, Isaac, and Jacob. They are God's *treasured* possession. They are to be a priestly kingdom, a holy nation that will show the radical love of God to the rest of the world. What an honored position they are given, to go from being slaves to becoming a priestly kingdom!

Words of Life and Freedom

As the people camp at the base of Mount Sinai, whose heights are covered in thick clouds of smoke, they are awed by the lightning and thunder that signal God's presence. Moses makes the three-hour climb up the mountain to hear what God has to say. "I am the LORD your God, who brought you out of the land of Egypt, out of the house of slavery; you shall have no other gods before me" (Exodus 20:2-3). And thus begins the Ten Commandments, or the Ten Words or Teachings, as they have also been called.

I think the Ten Commandments sometimes get neglected. Sometimes we can reduce them to simple moral principles or see them as outdated, irrelevant to our lives today and to the gospel message. We have probably even heard some Christians say that the Ten Commandments are just constructs of "the law" and that our lives should be built on grace and faith. Sadly, we don't tend to teach about them much anymore.

God delivers these commandments not to impose a burden but to offer a gift, an opportunity to grow in our relationship with God and with each other as God's children. Particularly during Lent, we as Christians are called to reflect on how our lives fail to embody these teachings and fall short of Christ's example.

The commandments come as a gift from God to help the people live as liberated people. What does this freedom mean for their life together? Do they get to live in the way that we often hear people talk about freedom today: "I should be able to do anything I want as long as I don't hurt anyone else"? What will shape their individual lives so they positively impact the whole community as worthy of the One who delivered them and with whom they are in covenant?

> *The commandments come as a gift from God to help the people live as liberated people.*

These words are not meant to be a new set of shackles for them or us. They are not meant to be read as moral finger-wagging. These covenants actually provide freedom for the Israelites (and us) to

47

live as God's treasured possession. They are a means of protecting the community of faith, who are no longer slaves, and opening a path to a flourishing life.

I asked my rule-loving daughter, now a high school teacher, why she believes rules are so important. "That's easy," she said. "Rules provide structure and create boundaries around the space you may play within. You know what's okay and what's not okay. You have lots of freedom within those boundaries."

That's true for the Israelites and us. Living within the covenantal boundaries set by God leads to abundant life and freedom. Stealing or coveting a neighbor's oxen, lawnmower, car, or spouse does not make for a happy and healthy community, an abundant life, or a good example to the world. It leads to a society where everyone is a law unto himself or herself and people live in fear of their neighbors rather than in the peace and harmony God intended. Which brings us back to the intention of Lent.

The Ten Commandments and Jesus

Lent, as you know, is a season that encompasses the forty days leading up to Easter. But why forty? Why not thirty or sixty? We spend forty days of reflection and penitence during Lent because Jesus fasted and faced temptations for forty days in the wilderness. As a matter of fact, the first Gospel reading of the first Sunday of Lent is always the story of Jesus's temptation in the wilderness. Have you noticed that Noah and his family watched the Flood waters rise for forty days? That the Israelites became impatient waiting for Moses to return from Mount Sinai with the stone tablets because he was gone for, you guessed it, forty days! That the Israelites wandered in the wilderness for forty years.

Some people speculate that these forties were chosen because they coincide with the number of weeks a woman carries a baby in her womb before new life appears. A new creation, new life, begins after the Flood. The former Hebrew slaves are born as newly freed people of the covenant when Moses finally appears with the two stone tablets. When they make their way into the Promised Land forty years later, it is the beginning of a new life in a settled existence.

I believe Jesus intentionally spends forty days in the wilderness so that his followers can see his connection to both the covenant made with Noah and especially the covenant made with the Israelites through Moses. In Matthew's Gospel, after Jesus successfully faces his temptation in the wilderness, he chooses his disciples, and the first sermon he offers is the Sermon on the Mount, where he interprets the law of Moses, the Ten Commandments, and says, "Do not think that I have come to abolish the Law or the Prophets; I have come not to abolish but to fulfill" (Matthew 5:17).

The Ten Commandments were inscribed onto two tablets, each with its own focus. The first four commandments are about maintaining a strong relationship with God. The last six address maintaining good relationships with our neighbors. Like boundary lines on a football field or basketball court, the commandments express the basic expectations for human behavior. They protect us from running out of bounds and from falling into habits or patterns of living that will bring harm to or destroy the community and lead to self-inflicted chaos and lack of life.

Jesus later reiterated the importance of the commandments. When a scribe asks which commandment is the most important, Jesus summarizes the first four commandments by citing Deuteronomy, "You shall love the LORD your God with all your heart and with all your soul and with all your might" (6:5). Then, quoting Leviticus 19:18, he encapsulates the second tablet given to Moses into this commandment: "You shall love your neighbor as yourself."

Jesus stresses that you cannot love God without loving your neighbor, and you cannot properly love your neighbor unless that love is rooted in one's love of God. Jesus unites the two tablets given to Moses, summarizing the whole of the gospel as love of

God and neighbor. The apostle Paul, trained as a rabbi, summed up the Law of Moses like this: "Love does no wrong to a neighbor; therefore, love is the fulfilling of the law" (Romans 13:10). As we read the covenant of Moses through the lens of the Christian faith, the Ten Commandments reveal themselves fully in the life of Jesus and the faithful witness of the church. Jesus's life shows us, as he feeds the hungry, heals the sick, and eats with outcasts, that we love God best when we love our neighbors well.

> **We love God best when we love our neighbors well.**

As we read the commandments, we see that they are not just a means unto themselves. They are meant to be less legalistic and more of a guidepost for how we should, and should not, live. Jesus taught us that a *liberated* life in community was one about loving God fully and loving neighbor—neither of which are expressly stated in the Ten Commandments. The Ten Commandments express the bare-minimum standards of how we should live. Jesus *shows us* the fullness of those standards.

Essentially, he is teaching, "Whatever else you may do, don't steal, don't covet, don't commit adultery, and don't murder. Don't tell lies about others. These are absolute boundaries." But that doesn't mean we come into right relationship with others (and with God) simply by adhering to these minimum standards. That's why Jesus teaches that, if we desire in our hearts to murder or commit adultery, even if we don't act on that desire, we have broken the spirit of God's law. We reach right relationships with others when we allow the boundaries of the Law to keep us on track toward what Paul describes as "the fruit of the Spirit": "love, joy, peace, patience, kindness, generosity, faithfulness, gentleness, and self-control" (Galatians 5:22-23).

God's Treasured Possession and
the Mending of God's Holy World

For those who are a treasured possession of God and called to be a priestly nation, good theology leads to good ethics and the mending of God's holy world. Adam Hamilton reminds us that "having no other gods but me" means that money, sex, and power will not worm their way onto the altar of our lives and won't be used to exploit others.[2] Keeping the Sabbath reminds us that we do not keep the world spinning on its axis; God does. We can take our hand off the keyboard, the vacuum cleaner, the pen, and the cell phone, and we will still be provided for. In his book, *Sabbath*, Wayne Muller reminds us that the Jewish Sabbath begins when the sun slips below the horizon. When that happens, it is time to put down the plow handle, not because all of our work is done, but because it is time.[3] We are no longer slaves in Egypt. We rest because God rested after creation. We rest because that is where we find delight in God and each other. In Sabbath rest, we are re-created.

Not bearing false witness teaches not just the behavior we should avoid but that we are to build up the community by speaking truthfully.

Not stealing and not coveting teach more than boundaries to avoid transgressing; they teach us to be content with what we have and trust in God to sustain us.

Not killing expresses more than an absolute prohibition; it teaches that all people are gifts created in God's image and likeness. Two centuries after Jesus's earthly lifetime, Jewish rabbis wrote commentaries, called the *Mishnah*, as they studied Scripture together (much as Christians do in our Bible studies). They wrestled with why God, who spoke an entire world into being, initially created only one man and one woman. The answer, they decided, was that God intended to show us the value of each life created in God's image. The rabbis wrote that Adam and Eve were created first to teach us that whoever destroys a single life is considered by Scripture to have destroyed an entire world; and whoever rescues a single life from the human family is considered to have saved an entire world.

When we adhere to the command to honor our parents, we acknowledge that we stand on the shoulders of those who have gone before. Even if you did not experience the example of loving parents, my hope is that there were those who filled in the gap and provided you with a strong foundation of life and faith. And if not, my prayer is that you have come to know God as the perfect parent—One who always loves you and desires the best for you. Many, including me, have known others who, outside the realm of their own families, provided examples of what it means to live out the covenant of the Ten Commandments.

Not only as I remember the lives that my parents lived, and as I try to live a life for my children that radiates the gospel love of God and neighbor, but also as I watch the lives and witness of those I have known closely in the church, I have also sometimes been reminded that staying within the boundaries God provides for us to care for others may require us to cross other boundaries.

Not too long ago, I officiated the funeral of a dear friend's husband. Bill was a pillar of our church a generation ago. He admittedly began life with all the prejudices that many of his generation did in the South. Still, his faith led him to overcome those prejudices and rise above the ingrained, systemic racism that was so prevalent then and that we see rearing its ugly head again today. Bill led a race relations committee in our church decades ago before others considered the notion. He co-taught and led a Disciple Bible Study with members of our church, Highland Park United Methodist, which is predominantly white, and the predominantly black Hamilton Park UMC in Dallas. He led the church to cross racial boundaries to advance racial reconciliation in Dallas. Bill also served people experiencing homelessness and the working poor. In staying within the limits God offers to God's people on Mount Sinai, Bill crossed the boundaries that typically separate wealthier neighborhoods from impoverished ones and divide God's children from each other.

One cold day as he was in conversation with a homeless man, Bill noticed the man wasn't wearing socks, so Bill took off his own socks and gave them to the man. Bill didn't know that another homeless man he was acquainted with was watching from a distance. As Bill turned to go home, the man who had been watching approached Bill and said, "Here, Bill, I have an extra pair of socks. You can take mine." Bill wanted to offer his knee-jerk reaction, which would have been to say, "Oh no, that's okay. I have lots of socks at home. You can keep yours." But instead, he realized that this man's gift came from a place of deep love and compassion formed within the radical, life- and love-giving boundaries of faith.

Bill allowed the man to show his love for neighbor (and God) by accepting the socks with deep gratitude. Bill was the type of man who would give you the shirt off his back and the socks off his feet. Like so many others whom you and I know, he lived the love of God and neighbor that Jesus lived and taught and that is encompassed in the Ten Commandments. It's a kind of love that brings blessing, healing, and new life to God's world. It's the kind of love that burns like a bush that is not being consumed, and it causes all who see it to want to turn aside out of curiosity to explore it more deeply. It's the kind of love that calls us all by name, draws us ever closer to the One who created us, and then sends us to confront the pharaohs of the world who keep God's children in bondage.

From the Foot of Mount Sinai
to the Foot of the Cross

Let's return to the foot of Mount Sinai with the wonder-struck people of God, awed by God's powerful presence. In that moment, they are eager to keep God's covenant because they are indebted to God for their freedom. They know that God has remembered them.

This Sinai moment is an exhilarating one. But it probably won't surprise you to know that, even before Moses comes down from the mountain, the people break their promise to worship Yahweh as their God. Worried that Moses has been gone a long time, they press Aaron, Moses's brother, to fashion a golden calf that they will worship as the god who brought them out of the land of Egypt (Exodus 32:1-4). Before they even begin their life together in freedom, they break the covenant, and God has an immediate response.

Their actions are so perverse that God contemplates abolishing the covenant made with Abraham and starting over with a new covenant made through Moses, making him a great nation (Exodus 32:7-10). In an almost comical scene (remember that these stories were initially handed down in oral form and meant to be engaging as well as instructive), Moses essentially talks God off the ledge, convincing God that these people should be given another try. God relents and carries on with these fallible, rebellious children of God. God relentlessly renews the covenants that humans break, remaining faithful in the face of human faithlessness.

> *God relentlessly renews the covenants that humans break, remaining faithful in the face of human faithlessness.*

We see the Israelites' breathtakingly rapid descent from the height of Sinai to the depth of the golden calf repeated even among Jesus's followers. Remember Peter, one of Jesus's inner circle of friends? He experiences his rapid fall in a single night. After vowing that he will follow Jesus to prison and even death (Luke 22:33-34), he denies even knowing Jesus, not once but three times (Luke 22:54-62). In the Israelites, in Peter, and in all those who came in between, we can see ourselves as would-be followers who inevitably will betray Jesus in thought, word, and deed. Like the awestruck Israelites at the foot of Sinai, they, and we, have great intentions. However, just as the Israelites' actions, and the betrayal by Peter, were not the end of either of their journeys, our own inevitable betrayals and covenant-breaking actions are not the end of ours either.

As the Israelites come to the end of their forty-year journey across the wilderness before entering the Promised Land, Moses gathers the people together to remind them of the importance of the covenant God made with them so many years before. Moses reminds them of the words that their faithful God had spoken. Most of those who had been adults in the wilderness die before reaching the Promised Land. Most of those present at the end of the journey had just been children, or not yet been born, at the beginning. Moses wants to impress upon them the importance of the words that God spoke to them. As he recounts the story of their exodus from slavery, he says these words about the Ten Words of the covenant:

> Hear, O Israel: The LORD is our God, the LORD alone. You shall love the LORD your God with all your heart and with all your soul and with all your might. Keep these words that I am commanding you today in your heart. Recite them to your children and talk about them when you are at home and when you are away, when you lie down and when you rise. Bind them as a sign on your hand, fix them as an emblem on your forehead, and write them on the doorposts of your house and on your gates.
>
> (Deuteronomy 6:4-9)

The Ten Words are so important that we should remind ourselves of them and talk about them. All the time. Deuteronomy 6:4 is called the *Shema*, named for its beginning word, which means "to hear" in Hebrew. Many Jewish people post these words on their doorposts in a mezuzah (a small container holding a tiny scroll of the Shema) as a reminder of the importance of these words. They seek to remember, as God remembers.

I attended a worship service not too long ago that began with this prayer:

> *Blessed Lord, who caused all holy Scriptures to be written for our learning: Grant us so to hear them, read, mark, learn, and inwardly digest them, that we may embrace and ever hold fast the blessed hope of everlasting life, which you have given us in our Savior Jesus Christ; who lives and reigns with you and the Holy Spirit, one God, for ever and ever. Amen.*[4]

The sermon that day was based on the Ten Commandments, and the preacher reminded us that when we see and hear these words of the covenant repeatedly, they are digested, they become a part of us, and we become a part of them. Something of every word we speak and think mysteriously nourishes our souls and bodies. That's how these words of Scripture should be for us.

The preacher continued, "May we hear, read, and mark these sacred words.... But unless we digest them, they are only squiggles on a page and make no difference....Only when we digest them and take them into our innermost selves, will they lead us to the foot of this mountain where we hear today, 'I am the One who is for you. Don't create an image of me and worship it because it can never replicate how much I love you....Don't ever obsess about anyone or anything because you will begin to build your life around something other than my love for you.'"[5]

These words of the covenant have the capacity to nourish us and feed us "until the world can no longer tell the difference between us and the words, and the Creative Power of the world will fill the world and bless every person and nation of the world."[6]

This has been God's intention from the beginning: that God's words would come to life in each of us, nourishing us, filling us, and restoring our image as those made in the image of the Creator of life and love. God reiterated this intention in the covenant at Sinai and later at the cross of Jesus, whose words and life mysteriously nourish our souls and bodies. May we digest every morsel of every word and story that leads us to life through him.

CHAPTER FOUR

David:
An Eternal Covenant

Thus says the LORD of hosts: I took you from the pasture, from following the sheep to be prince over my people Israel, and I have been with you wherever you went and have cut off all your enemies from before you, and I will make for you a great name, like the name of the great ones of the earth. And I will appoint a place for my people Israel and will plant them, so that they may live in their own place and be disturbed no more, and evildoers shall afflict them no more, as formerly, from the time that I appointed judges over my people Israel, and I will give you rest from all your enemies. Moreover, the LORD declares to you that the LORD will make you a house. When your days are fulfilled and you lie down with your ancestors, I will raise up your offspring after you, who shall come forth from your body, and I will establish his kingdom. He shall build a house for my name, and I will establish the throne of his kingdom forever. . . . Your house and your kingdom shall be made sure forever before me; your throne shall be established forever.

(2 Samuel 7:8b-13, 16)

What image comes to mind when you first think of David? Is it of the brave young boy ferociously circling a slingshot in the air, hurling a stone at the head of the giant Philistine, Goliath? Or maybe you think of the small and ruddy-complected youth who was summoned from tending the family's sheep. Or perhaps the image pressed most deeply in your mind is of the adult

King David spying the beautiful (and married) Bathsheba bathing on her rooftop—and all of the passion, heartache, and consequences that follow in the wake of his poor decisions that began on that day. Maybe your first thought of David is that he was described as "a man after [God's] own heart" (1 Samuel 13:14; Acts 13:22). Least likely to come first to anyone's mind, but of most importance to the history of Israel and Christianity, is the story of God creating a covenant with David.

The covenants with Noah, Abraham, and Moses are legendary. They are easily recalled. A flood ends with a new creation and a rainbow. A childless, elderly couple *goes* to the land that God will show them, and they are blessed with a son whose descendants become as numerous as the desert's grains of sand. Those descendants, all twelve tribes of them, are delivered from slavery to become a priestly nation that is to follow God's ordinances—and to be a light to other nations. Each covenant involves the promise of God's fidelity—God's faithfulness. And what of the covenant made with David? What does it offer to the people of Israel? to us as Christians? And how is this covenant significant to our Lenten journey and Jesus's journey to the cross? Let's take a look.

The Journey from Moses to David

To fully grasp the meaning and weight of God's covenant with David, we will take a brief glimpse of his life—how he became king and how his life and this covenant intersect with the season of Lent and Jesus. But it would also be helpful to understand a little history leading up to the story of David. As you might guess, his life story is inseparable from the life story of Israel.

Once Moses leads the Israelites to the edge of the Promised Land, Joshua, Moses's successor, is bequeathed with the responsibility for leading the people to conquer and inhabit Canaan. As you can imagine, the process is long and arduous. It culminates in eleven family clans living in various areas apportioned to them; the tribe of Levi is dispersed among the others to act as priests. The twelve tribes function as a loose confederation, and after the death of Joshua, "judges" are appointed by God to rule over them.

The word "judge" in Hebrew is *sopet*, which can mean to "decide," "judge," "rule," "govern," or "deliver." Judges were appointed to maintain harmonious relations between the Israelites, settle legal disputes, and decide justly for the poor, widows, orphans, and aliens in the land. Judges would also lead armies into battle against Israel's enemies or oppressors. The Book of Judges gives us stories of twelve judges who ruled between Israel's entry into Canaan and the establishment of a monarchy in Israel. Many of these stories reveal repeating cycles of unfaithfulness, in the form of idolatry and social and moral decay, followed by oppression from enemies, repentance, and deliverance.

> **The stories in Judges set the stage for the people's desire for a monarchy.**

The stories in Judges set the stage for the people's desire for a monarchy. While some Scripture seems to condemn having a king rule over Israel—Samuel explicitly warns them against a human ruler—the stories of chaos and human faithlessness, with God repeatedly raising up leaders to rescue the people from enemies in the Book of Judges, also help us understand why the Israelites wanted a strong and permanent leader.

Why is the story of Israel's greatest king encompassed in two books named after someone else? Samuel lives in a time of heightened internal and external turmoil. Internally, the people feel spiritually barren. The sons of their chief priest, Eli, are morally bankrupt, offering a poor example of priestly leadership. Externally, the people are continually attacked by their hostile neighbors.

Into this environment arrives Samuel, who is dedicated to God's service as a boy by his mother, Hannah, in gratitude for

God's answer to her prayers to end her childlessness. Samuel is the answer to both the people's prayers to end their spiritual barrenness and a mother's prayer to end her physical one. After growing up under the tutelage of Eli, Samuel becomes an extraordinary priest, judge, and prophet who leads the people back to God and keeps them safe from their enemies. But as he grows older, no one emerges from his sons as a worthy successor. Wanting to be like the other nations that seem stronger and better able to defend themselves, the people demand a king.

While Samuel feels rejected by the people, God reminds him that it is God's leadership, not Samuel's, they are rejecting. Samuel warns the people what their choice will mean. A king will conscript their sons for military service and their daughters to care for his home. He will tax them. He will take the best of their fields and vineyards. The people are undeterred. God assures Samuel that he will still have a role as prophet and priest, leading him to anoint the first king of Israel with oil.

Tall, strong, and handsome, Saul looks like the perfect candidate for king, at first. And for a time, it seems he is a stellar choice. Saul wins many victories over Israel's enemies but soon becomes infatuated with his power. Hubris sets in. Saul begins disobeying God's orders, preferring his own insights and military tactics (1 Samuel 15:10-24). Not only does he dangerously cross strict boundaries God has put in place for him, Saul even usurps Samuel's role as priest (1 Samuel 13:8-14). God decides it is time for Samuel to begin the search process for a new king. Enter the unsuspecting boy, David.

From Shepherd Boy to the Anointed One of Israel

With Saul still occupying the throne, God directs Samuel to travel to Bethlehem to the house of Jesse. There he will anoint the future king from among Jesse's sons. It's a risky proposition for Samuel. Saul will surely have Samuel killed if he learns of this scheme. But Samuel follows God's instructions in faith (1 Samuel 16:1-3).

One by one, each of the seven sons of Jesse stands before Samuel. The first is so impressive that Samuel is convinced this tall, handsome man must be God's choice. However, God reminds him that "the LORD does not see as mortals see; they look on the outward appearance, but the LORD looks on the heart" (1 Samuel 16:6-7). God rejects each candidate in turn.

"Are all your sons here?" asks Samuel. Jesse explains that one more, the youngest, is in the field, tending the sheep. "Bring him here," Samuel commands (1 Samuel 16:11, paraphrased).

In walks young David, with the smell of grass and sheep still lingering in his hair and clothes. This unassuming boy is God's choice for Israel's king, not because of his ruddy complexion and beautiful eyes, but because of the condition of his heart. Samuel pulls out his horn of oil and anoints David with it. Immediately, "the spirit of the LORD came mightily upon David from that day forward" (1 Samuel 16:13).

Being anointed with oil conveyed God's blessing. Kings have been anointed with oil since the time of Saul. After the death of Queen Elizabeth II, televised remembrances of her coronation showed her anointing (concealed by a canopy) by the Archbishop of Canterbury. It is a sacred moment in which a monarch assumes the mantle of responsibility and feels the weight of duty to obey God's desires and ordinances as they pertain to leading the people.

God has anointed you, too. Some ministers or priests anoint the forehead of those being baptized with oil, making the sign of the cross. Even if you weren't anointed with oil at your baptism, you are set apart for God's service just the same. Regardless of our professions, we are called to live into our roles in life knowing we are anointed, feeling the mantle and weight of our duty to serve God and our messiah (which means "anointed"), to serve all whom we meet in our life's journey.

While David has received this anointing, it will be some time before he is actually crowned king. At first, he serves in Saul's court, and Saul loves him—until he doesn't. David's miraculous defeat of Goliath elevates him to superhero status among the Israelites. Jealousy begins to burn in Saul's heart against David until it turns into a murderous rage. Many believe that Saul suffered not only from jealousy but from mental illness as well. David flees from Saul's court until Saul and his sons are killed in battle against the Philistines (1 Samuel 31). Yet David holds no grudge against Saul. Instead, he mourns for Saul and his son Jonathan, even writing a song of lament that is one of the Bible's earliest poems. From this song comes the phrase, "How the mighty have fallen!" (2 Samuel 1:19).

David, at the age of thirty, is installed as king, first over Judah and later over all of Israel. He remains on the throne for forty years. David soon makes Jerusalem the capital city and brings the ark of the covenant (which housed the tablets given to Moses) there permanently.

The Covenant: I Will Build You a House

And this is where we come to what one of my former seminary professors calls the most crucial passage in the Hebrew Scriptures (or Old Testament): 2 Samuel, chapter 7. The passage cited at the beginning of this chapter contains the covenant God makes with David. This covenant has shaped the understanding of Jesus's followers—both his Jewish disciples and then Christians—as the Messiah, God's anointed.

David has been a great king. He has brought peace and stability to Israel that now functions, not as a confederation of tribes but as a nation with its own land (fully realizing God's covenant with Abraham). David lives in a beautiful house built of the finest cedar. It doesn't seem right to him that the ark of the covenant should still be housed in a tent, as it was in the days in the wilderness at

Sinai, while he lives in a mansion. After all, the people understood the ark to contain the very presence of God. Shouldn't God have a nicer dwelling than David? So David tells his prophet, Nathan (remember, prophets are to speak for God, providing counsel and caution for the king), of his intention to build God a house. Initially, Nathan agrees that this is a splendid idea.

But that night, God's voice comes to Nathan with a different message:

> "Go and tell my servant David: Thus says the LORD: Are **you** the one to build **me** a house to live in? I have not lived in a house since the day I brought up the people of Israel from Egypt to this day, but I have been moving about in a tent and a tabernacle. Wherever I have moved about among all the people of Israel, did I **ever** speak a word with any of the tribal leaders of Israel . . . saying, 'Why have you not built me a house of cedar?'"
>
> (2 Samuel 7:5-7, emphasis added)

Gracious as David's offer may sound, God doesn't want or need a house. In refusing to be limited to a name that humans could summon, the God who told Moses, "I am who I am" (Exodus 3:14), doesn't wish to be confined to one place or domesticated by David. God has always been, and will always be, moving among the people of God, leading, directing, and protecting them (not the other way around). As John's Gospel reminds us, God may move where God pleases (John 3:8).

> *God has always been, and will always be, moving among the people of God, leading, directing, and protecting them.*

God instructs Nathan to remind David that God has been with him since he was a mere shepherd; that God has delivered all of David's enemies into his hand; and that God will make his name great.

These words would have a familiar ring if you were Jewish and steeped in Hebrew Scriptures. Your ears would perk up because you would know that, just before God makes a covenant with Abraham, God reminds *him* of what God has done for him, and then promises to make of him "a great name." You would recall that, before God makes a covenant with Moses and the newly freed tribes of Israel encamped at Sinai, God reminds *them* of what God has done and will do for them ("I bore you on eagles' wings and brought you to myself.... You shall be my treasured possession...a priestly kingdom and a holy nation," Exodus 19:4-6). No doubt that Nathan, when hearing God's instructions about what he is to say to David, senses what God is about to do next: David will become the recipient of a covenant—an heir, if you will, to God's promises to Abraham and Moses.

David has had to fight for the hard-won security that Israel enjoys. God promises to appoint a place where the people—through God's protection, not just David's—can live undisturbed by their enemies. Then God basically says, "You're not going to build *me* a house; I will make *you* a house."

What does God mean by this? *House* can also mean "dynasty," which becomes apparent in God's next words to David. God promises that David will be the first in a royal dynasty that will last forever. But did you notice what else God promises in the passage establishing the covenant with David? (Take a quick look at the verses that follow the passage at the beginning of this chapter.) God essentially acknowledges that David's human descendants will not always be faithful: "When he commits iniquity, I will punish him"—not *if* Israel breaks faith but *when*. In the next breath, God promises, "I will not take my steadfast love from him" (2 Samuel 7:14-15).

David's Covenant and Judaism

In keeping with God's promise, David has a son, Solomon, who builds a house to honor and worship the God who brought the Israelites out of Egypt, the God who plucked David from the fields to become king. But God's promise that David's descendants will sit on the throne of Israel *forever* is good news that extends to the king and the whole people. The words God speaks to David provide comfort and hope to the Jewish people four centuries after David's time, when the Temple was destroyed, and the people were taken into exile in a foreign land.

In those days, with no Temple in which to worship, they remember that God doesn't need a house to be present among them. God moves with them and among them. They can remember the promise that, wherever they find themselves, God will never remove God's steadfast love from them. They receive hope through this covenant that they will one day return home and that God will raise a descendant of David to lead Israel once more.

Scholars believe 1 and 2 Samuel were once a single book, which took its final form during the Babylonian Exile. You can see how this covenant helped the people of Israel cling to hope while waiting for their return to their homeland.

Exile and displacement have been recurring events in the history of the Jewish people. The Romans scattered Jews from Jerusalem after crushing a revolt and destroying the Second Temple in 70 CE. In the year they dispatched Columbus on his voyage of discovery, Ferdinand and Isabella of Spain expelled Jews from their land. The Russian czars confined Jews to certain areas of their empire, where violent persecution drove many to emigrate to America.

God's promise to David did not mean that the people would not endure an exile in Babylon, just as the promise to Abraham did not mean there would be no time of slavery in Egypt. But the promises meant the people could count on God to remember.

Even after the destruction of Solomon's Temple. Even after the Roman destruction of the Temple that Jesus knew. Even after the Holocaust, which is still within the living memory of some survivors.

> ## *God hears us too. God remembers.*

Aren't there times in our lives when we feel a bit like those exiled in Babylon, when we feel uprooted and abandoned? Or when we wonder where God is because we had this small box we kept God in, or this image of whom God was supposed to be, and we found that God wasn't as small as we imagined. We, too, can cling to this covenant. We, too, can remember that God is always with us no matter how alone we feel. God will never take God's love away from us but will always seek to lead us home, and remind us that David's son, God's Son, reigns over his kingdom *forever*. God heard the cries of the people in Egypt and of the exiles in Babylon. God hears us too. God remembers.

David's Covenant and Christianity

As noted earlier, God's covenant with David has shaped Christians' understanding of Jesus as the Messiah. Second Samuel chapter 7 provides the backdrop for multiple passages pointing to Jesus as the Messiah. Since the Babylonian Exile, Israel had been waiting for God's promise that "a shoot shall come out of the stump of Jesse, and a branch shall grow out of his roots" (Isaiah 11:1). The words of the angel Gabriel to Mary declare that God will give to the son born to her "the throne of his ancestor David. He will reign over the house of Jacob *forever*, and of his kingdom there will be no end" (Luke 1:32-33, emphasis added).

The genealogies at the beginning of the Gospels of Matthew and Luke, as well as the angel's appearance to Joseph

(Matthew 1:20-22), confirm that Jesus is a descendant of David through his earthly father. The Gospels also tell us that people often addressed Jesus as "Son of David," in apparent recognition that he was the one God would raise up from the root of Jesse to rule forever, in keeping with God's covenant.

But one of the most profound scriptural affirmations of Jesus as Messiah, the Son of David, comes from Jesus himself through a prophetic action. As he makes his triumphal entry into Jerusalem on what we have come to call Palm Sunday, Jesus is intentionally mounted on the back of a donkey. His actions speak volumes about how he wishes to reveal his identity to the people following him. As Matthew tells us:

> This took place to fulfill what had been spoken through the prophet [Zechariah]:

> "Tell the daughter of Zion,
> Look, your king is coming to you,
>   humble, and mounted on a donkey,
>   and on a colt, the foal of a donkey."
>   (Matthew 21:4-5, quoting Zechariah 9:9)

Zechariah's oracle envisioned God reestablishing the rule of God's Davidic leader. When Jesus rides into Jerusalem on a donkey, the ecstatic crowds know what this prophetic action means. Could this be the one they have been waiting for? They enthusiastically wave palm branches as Jesus travels along the road, shouting, "Hosanna to the Son of David! Blessed is the one who comes in the name of the Lord!"

But God ultimately fulfills this promise to David in an unexpected way—not only raising someone from David's lineage but fulfilling that role in God's own person. In Jesus, the story comes full circle. As you may remember, God originally was understood to be Israel's king—one of the qualities that set Israel apart from other nations—until the people clamored for a human king. While human kings repeatedly fail to remain faithful to God's covenants, in the coming of Jesus, we see God keeping the promise to allow a human king while simultaneously restoring God as the ruler of Israel and all humankind.

David the Covenant Breaker

Despite God's promises and everything God has done for him, David fails to keep faith. After he sees Bathsheba bathing on her rooftop, he summons her to his palace and begins an affair with her—even though Uriah, her husband, who is also one of David's loyal officers, is off fighting a war for David. When Bathsheba informs the king she's pregnant, David tries to conceal his transgression from public knowledge. When David realizes that her husband will learn the truth, he orders his general to send Uriah to the front lines and leave him exposed to enemy fire, knowing he'll be killed. While God has been faithful to David, David manages to break the covenantal commandments against coveting, stealing, adultery, murder, and false witness in one fell swoop.[1]

David remains in denial about his sin (his unspoken motto becomes "out of sight, out of mind") until his astute prophet, Nathan, notices a stench coming from the palace walls and confronts him. Today, we might call the prophet's action an intervention. Through Nathan, David is forced to face his own brokenness.

Looking Inside Ourselves

It's fitting that Psalm 51, one of the first readings that begin the Lenten season on Ash Wednesday, is attributed to the very human David. If it wasn't composed by David himself, it was certainly written about his contrition in the wake of his murderous taking of Bathsheba. Ash Wednesday developed as a day of penitence to mark the beginning of Lent. On this day we also recall our mortality, as we remember "from dust we were created and to dust we shall return,"[2] and we wait upon the Lord for a renewing spirit. We pray, as David did, "Create in me a clean heart, O God, and put a new and right spirit within me" (Psalm 51:10).

During Ash Wednesday and throughout the Lenten season, we put aside the sins and failures of the past in the light of who we are yet to become by the grace of God. This is a season of reflection, a time to take an honest look inside ourselves, at the condition of our hearts—to see where there might be some room for improvement—and renew our commitment to following Jesus on his journey to the cross.

> *During Ash Wednesday and throughout the Lenten season, we put aside the sins and failures of the past in the light of who we are yet to become by the grace of God.*

Psalm 51 invites us to look inside ourselves, to seek what God desires: "truth in the inward being" (v. 6). Sometimes we want to avoid looking inside because it's too painful. But the very first lines of this confessional psalm invoke God's promise to David and to us: "Have mercy on me, O God, *according to your steadfast love*" (emphasis added).

When I was a little girl, I had a teddy bear that I loved. I took that little brown bear with me everywhere. I even slept with it. One day my cousin came to play, and during our playtime, as we were contemplating what we should do next, she said, "I have a great idea! Why don't we wash your teddy bear?"

I wholeheartedly embraced the bad idea of washing the teddy bear. My cousin and I stuck Teddy in the bathroom sink in our basement and lathered him up with shaving cream. Soon, Teddy was a soapy mess with brown dye bleeding profusely through the foam and into the sink. What had seemed inspired now proved to be a huge mistake. Fearing how my parents would react to this debacle, I snuck upstairs, snatched a few pairs of pajamas, wrapped them tightly around Teddy, placed him in a doll cradle, and stashed him in the farthest recess of my dark closet.

Then I conveniently "forgot" about him. I treated the problem of my teddy bear much like David did with Bathsheba and Uriah. Teddy was out of sight and out of mind. I didn't want to look inside the back of my closet to confront the mess I had made. Looking back, I must have thought that if I ignored the problem, it would resolve itself. I wish I had known a little about chemistry at age five. For we all know what happens when you leave damp chemistry cultures in a dark place. Teddy was left fermenting in that closet for I don't know how long—weeks perhaps.

What I learned about being afraid to look inside is what David learned, that trying to hide a problem only compounds it. Soon, a stench emerged from the closet, but I didn't notice it because I had been living in the stench. However, my astute mother, like Nathan, did notice and sought out its cause.

When confronted with the evidence (brown pajamas, wet stinking bear) I used an excuse that is old as Adam and Eve: I blamed my cousin for the whole affair!

This is the human condition—wanting to avoid taking an honest look at our failures and casting blame on others for them. That may be expected from a five-year-old, but not mature people of faith. And that is what I love about David. David's response to Nathan is one reason why the Scriptures describe him as a man after God's own heart. Once he sees how grievous his behavior has been, he doesn't deny it, he doesn't make excuses, and he doesn't shift blame. He owns up to his rotten behavior: "I have sinned against the LORD" (2 Samuel 12:13). With a contrite heart, he repents of his actions, and Nathan assures him, "Now the LORD has put away your sin."

It's worth noting here that David experiences the natural consequences of his poor decisions, of breaking faith with God. It is just as God had warned in the covenant: "When he commits iniquity, I will punish him." David's actions make for extreme family dysfunction. His daughter, Tamar, is raped by her half-brother Amnon. Despite his anger when he discovers what happened, Scripture tells us that David does not punish Amnon because he loved him and Amnon was his firstborn (2 Samuel 13).

I wonder if David hesitated to confront Amnon the way Nathan confronted him because he believed he lacked moral footing given his past. Because David fails to act on Tamar's behalf, her fully biological brother, Absalom, avenges the violation of his sister by arranging for the murder of Amnon (2 Samuel 13:23-29) and plots to usurp David's throne. Absalom is killed by David's troops during the uprising, which is heartbreaking for David (2 Samuel 15; 18).

The text of 2 Samuel 12:14 attributes the death of David and Bathsheba's child, conceived in their adulterous relationship, to David's actions. However, we might read that and wonder: Does an all-merciful God function that way? Or does David, torn by guilt over his actions, believe that the innocent baby's death was God's action and not just coincidence? We sometimes torment ourselves, refusing to forgive ourselves when we break faith with God. We wonder how God could forgive us even though we are remorseful.

And yet, God forgives us, just as God forgave David from the moment he confessed his sin. God kept the promise of an unbreakable bond of love. Nothing we can ever do will ever separate us from God's love. As we continue in our story of the interactions between God and human beings, we will see this pattern repeat over and over. Despite human faithlessness, God continually reaffirms love for us. Through God's love and forgiveness, we are freed to live as models of that forgiveness, and in John the Baptist's phrase, to bear "fruits worthy of repentance" (Luke 3:8a).

The Scripture readings for Lent, especially Psalm 51, offer us the opportunity to allow God to shine a light in the dark, damp closets of our hearts, and help us clean up the mess we've left behind. Encouraging us to own up to our own rotten attitudes and behaviors (the biblical word for this is *sin*), these readings call us to grow up in our faith, take responsibility for our failures, and say "I'm sorry" to the One who wants more than anything to restore us to the relationship for which we were created, a relationship that brings joy, allowing us to move past our failures and grow into what we are yet to be by the grace of God.

In recent years, I have been amazed to watch the remarkable fruit borne by truth and reconciliation commissions that work to help nations move beyond the trauma inflicted on their people by great moral sins. In South Africa, such a commission documented injustices under the old system of racial apartheid. In Rwanda, they documented genocide committed by one ethnic group against another. In Argentina and Uruguay, they documented the torture and murder of political opponents by the government. In each case, the commission's purpose was not to assign blame or administer punishment. It was to bring the harsh, painful truth out of the dark closet and into the light—to name and confront sin so that healing and reconciliation can begin. Confession, as the saying goes, is good for the soul. It is good for relationships. It is good for us, and it was good for David.

Lent reminds us to look inside. It also reminds us of our mortality. The essayist and novelist Anna Quindlen says she thinks that knowledge of our mortality is the greatest gift God ever gives us.[3] I agree—it makes life more precious. When I worked on staff at a large church, we encountered death almost daily, and it has struck me that it makes no difference whether you live to be 27 or 97: Life is short and fragile and precious. It is too short to live in bitterness and anger. It is too short to live in hiding and blaming. Remember "you are dust / and to dust you shall return" (Genesis 3:19).

One of my favorite preachers and writers, Barbara Brown Taylor, says that until the last several years, she had always heard that sentence as a negative comment on flesh—and then September 11 happened. "No one had to go to church for ashes," she wrote. "Television screens were full of ashes. The air in Manhattan was full of ashes. Hearts around the world were full of ashes."[4] During the aftermath, Taylor heard a New York City Port Authority official interviewed on the radio. He described relief workers sifting through the powdered debris on the ground, carrying two handfuls at a time over to a tarp where they searched for anything recognizably human.

What struck him most, he said, was the workers' reverence for what they carried in their hands. "It's nothing but ashes," he said, "and yet you should see how they touch it." Taylor reminds us that the good news of the Lenten season is more about the holiness of ashes than the weakness of our flesh, for God chose to breathe life into ashes and called it "very good." The ashes pressed onto our foreheads at the beginning of Lent are not curses, but blessings, "announcing God's undying love of dust no matter what shape it is in."[5]

What I learned as a five-year-old is that because I had hidden my mistake and covered it up for so long, my teddy bear had become completely contaminated. It was beyond a good "airing out." It was beyond salvaging, saving, or restoring. It had become toxic, and in order to protect our health it had to be discarded. We lived in the country and didn't have garbage service, so the teddy bear had to be burned—reduced to ashes.

Soon, on Good Friday, we will have the opportunity to take an honest look inside the tomb of the broken, lifeless body of Jesus, our king whose kingdom shall have no end. Then, thankfully, we can follow Jesus's friends and look with them inside the empty tomb on Easter morning. The good news is that we, like David, are never beyond God's ability and desire to restore, heal, and raise us from the ashes of our past failures. We, too, can be people after God's own heart. We can cling with hope to the covenant God made with David—the covenant fulfilled in the Son of David whose birth was announced to Mary by the angel Gabriel ("You will conceive in your womb and bear a son....He will be great and will be called the Son of the Most High, and the Lord God will give to him the throne of his ancestor David. He will reign over the house of Jacob forever, and of his kingdom there will be no end," Luke 1:31-33).

> **The good news is that we, like David, are never beyond God's ability and desire to restore, heal, and raise us from the ashes of our past failures.**

We can cling to the covenant God made with David, and that was fulfilled by the Son of David, who was enthusiastically greeted by the palm-waving crowds on Palm Sunday, shouting, "Hosanna to the Son of David! Blessed is the one who comes in the name of the Lord!" (Matthew 21:9). We can cling to—we can remember—the covenant God made with David, as we look to the cross on which the Son of David, the Son of the Most High, the Christ, the Anointed One gave his life that we might have new life and become a new creation—over and over again.

May you know with certainty that the God who remembered Noah, Abraham, Moses, and David remembers you. May you know with certainty that the Son of David, the Son of God, will never remove his steadfast love *from* you. For his cross stands as a promise of his eternal love *for* you and all of God's children.

CHAPTER FIVE

From Jeremiah to Jesus:
The Covenant of the Heart

The days are surely coming, says the LORD, when I will make a new covenant with the house of Israel and the house of Judah. It will not be like the covenant that I made with their ancestors when I took them by the hand to bring them out of the land of Egypt—a covenant that they broke, though I was their husband, says the LORD. But this is the covenant that I will make with the house of Israel after those days, says the LORD: I will put my law within them, and I will write it on their hearts, and I will be their God, and they shall be my people. No longer shall they teach one another or say to each other, "Know the LORD," for they shall all know me, from the least of them to the greatest, says the LORD, for I will forgive their iniquity and remember their sin no more.

(Jeremiah 31:31-34)

After almost forty years, I can still recall this moment as clearly as if it happened yesterday. Driving down the ten-lane, almost always congested freeway that encircles Dallas, I felt a sudden emptiness in my soul and an ache in my heart. Something was wrong. It had been gnawing at me for some time, but I just then stopped to consider why, when everything seemed to be going so right in my life, my spirit seemed dull and lifeless. Four years post-college, I had a job I loved teaching high school students. I led four academic classes per day, and as the cherry on top of the sundae, I directed a fifty-five-member dance team full of enthusiastic, creative, and talented teenage girls.

As you can imagine, there was never a dull moment. In addition, my incredible roommate was a good friend from our dancing days in college. We would often find ourselves howling with laughter while choreographing tap dances on the linoleum floor of our apartment's tiny kitchen for my team's spring shows. I also had a family who loved me dearly, and many close friendships. What else could a young, single girl want? Yet something was clearly missing.

And then it struck me: Everything was as it should be—except in my spiritual life. I began attending a wonderful church not long after moving to Dallas, but at some point, I had stopped going. I couldn't even remember when. Perhaps it was during a time of trying to juggle the demands of planning curriculum, leading department meetings, grading papers, and conducting late-night rehearsals. But I realized it had been a *long* time since my heart and soul felt full and satisfied. It had been far too long since I had participated in Communion, picked up a Bible, read any devotional material, or served others in the community. I had been extremely disciplined about stretching and conditioning myself physically and intellectually but had spent zero time or effort tending my relationship with God and serving others.

In this moment on the freeway, I realized that I had forgotten about God. I had neglected the most important relationship in my life, and that neglect manifested itself in the depths of my heart and soul, and in the way I thought (or didn't) about others. Thankfully, God hadn't forgotten about me. God was present on that freeway, softly whispering into the depths of my heart, waiting patiently for me to return and tend the relationship with the One in whom "we live and move and have our being" (Acts 17:28). God was ready to reboot our relationship even when I had unconsciously turned away. And the reboot began on a freeway with God speaking to my heart.

The condition of my heart before God intervened, sadly, is part of the human condition. God cares about the condition of our hearts. After all, as Jeremiah envisioned, the heart is the vessel upon which the new covenant will be inscribed. The condition of our hearts matters. With the coming of the Word made flesh, our hearts have the capacity to become pliable and ready to receive what God, through Jesus, has prepared for us: intimacy with God and with each other.

We desire intimacy in our closest relationships, whether that's with our spouses, children, siblings, or God. We long to be loved, unconditionally, for who we are. We want to know that those we love most can look into our hearts and love us at our best and our worst. Their love spurs us to reciprocate that love. It makes us want to be our best. Recognizing the depth of God's love for us can do the same.

But as we have seen so far in this "salvation story," we human beings have failed repeatedly in our efforts to regain the intimate, innocent, trusting relationship originally enjoyed between God and Adam and Eve. Our fear holds us back from trusting fully. Our self-centeredness isolates us from God and from our fellow children of the Creator. Our selfish desires, born from lack of faith, lead us to turn material things into idols. Time after time, God responds through covenants that remind us of God's faithfulness and invite us into the intimate relationship that God desires for us—and that our own hearts crave but cannot achieve.

Now, centuries after David's time, God announces a new covenant that will do what we have failed to do on our own: to make God's Law more than something we simply read and learn, but part and parcel of who we are. Through this covenant, in which God is the unilateral actor, we can know and trust God fully as God's law of love is inscribed on our hearts, radiating from the center of our being. In Jesus, we see Jeremiah's prophecy come true. And in the process, as John's Gospel explains it, God empowers us to be transformed through love and to participate in the renewal of the world—to be not just beloved by God but to become *of* God.

> *God empowers us to be transformed through love and to participate in the renewal of the world—to be not just beloved by God but to become of God.*

One of my favorite roles as a minister is to officiate weddings and offer premarital counseling to couples preparing not only for their wedding day, but more importantly, for a lifetime of marriage. I always ask them, "What do you love most about the person you are about to marry? What is it about this person that makes you want to spend the rest of your life with him or her?" Almost always, I hear responses like these:

"He always puts my needs before his."

"She is thoughtful, loving, and kind to everyone she meets."

"When my mother was dying, he was my rock and was always there for me."

"He brings out the best in me and makes me want to be a better person."

"Our relationship with our families and God is important to us both."

Most of the couples I counsel have lived long enough to know that true love, the kind that inspires a lifetime of faithfulness that can carry a couple through the most challenging circumstances, is more than a romantic feeling. Mature love that keeps persons bound in a covenant relationship is comprised of intentional actions, like those the apostle Paul spelled out in his first letter to the church in Corinth: "Love is patient; love is kind; love is not envious or boastful or arrogant or rude. It does not insist on its own way; it is not irritable; it keeps no record of wrongs; it does not rejoice in wrongdoing but rejoices in the truth" (1 Corinthians 13:4-6).

Paul didn't write these words to couples about to enter a marriage covenant. He wrote them to a church that was imploding due to its members' arrogant, selfish, childish behavior. But his words apply not only to churches, but to all relationships (even marriages). Those of us who have been married for more than a week can attest that it's impossible to live out this kind of mature love day in and day out without relying on the infinite supply of love and forgiveness offered to us by our Creator and our Christ, for "God is love" (1 John 4:8). If we expect to continue to see the same love reflected in the eyes of the person we covenant to stay with through richer or poorer, in sickness and in health, till death do us part, both parties have to be intentional in drawing on the love, faithfulness, patience, and forgiveness of God.

Sadly, some of the same couples I've joined together in marriage, whose futures seemed so promising, who at that moment *were* genuinely committed to intentionally loving one another for a lifetime, end up breaking their covenant vows. Either one or both of them forget about the intentionality of showing loving behaviors toward each other, and they drift apart through benign neglect. Sometimes those vows are broken through abusive behaviors. Or one may stray by being unfaithful.

One of the most consistent themes in the story of the people who wrestle with God—starting with Abraham's descendants and continuing through us—is human inconsistency. And the most consistent theme is God's faithfulness in the face of human infidelity. Throughout our story, we see the people repeatedly breaking the covenant, beginning with the worshipping of a golden calf while Moses is on the mountain receiving God's Law.

You may have noticed in the passage above that the Scripture refers to God as Israel's husband. This isn't the first time God has been compared to a husband and Israel to an unfaithful bride. The prophet Hosea, active during the time of the divided kingdom of Israel (more about that later), speaks out against the Northern Kingdom on behalf of God. The people are worshipping Baal, a Canaanite fertility god (Hosea 4:12-14), and the rich and powerful have exploited the poor and weak (Hosea 12:7). Hosea, giving voice to God, describes Israel in this way:

> [She] decked herself with her rings and jewelry
>> and went after her lovers
>> and forgot me, says the LORD.

> Therefore, I will now allure her
>> and bring her into the wilderness
>> and speak tenderly to her . . .

> There she shall respond as in the days of her youth,
>> as at the time when she came out of the land of Egypt.

> On that day, says the LORD, you will call me "my husband," and no longer . . . "my Baal" . . .

> I will make for you a covenant on that day . . . and I will abolish the bow, the sword, and war from the land. . . . And I will take you for my wife forever; I will take you for my wife in righteousness and in justice, in steadfast love and in mercy. I will take you for my wife in faithfulness, and you shall know the LORD.
>> (Hosea 2:13b-14, 15b-16, 18-20)

God instructs Hosea not only to speak prophetically against Israel's adultery using these words; he also is to live prophetically, showing the people of God how they have been unfaithful. Hosea marries a prostitute, Gomer (Hosea 1:2-3), who is unfaithful to him. But God instructs Hosea to continue to be faithful and lovingly pursue her, just as God will continue to lovingly pursue Israel despite her unfaithfulness. Hosea prophecies to the Northern Kingdom that, by worshipping Baal, they have acted as adulterous wives and as rebellious children (Hosea 11:1-11). However, as we can see through Hosea's actions and words, God will not abandon or break covenant with them. Instead, God will continue to seek ways to renew the relationship with Israel.

Just before they cross into the Promised Land, Moses's successor, Joshua, recounts to the people everything God has done for them and calls on them to renew the covenant made at Sinai. "If you are unwilling to serve the LORD, choose this day whom you will serve," Joshua tells them (Joshua 24:15). The people enthusiastically affirm their commitment to God. And then Joshua issues both a warning and a prediction: "You cannot serve the LORD, for he is a holy God" (24:19). The people insist they will serve the Lord. So Joshua erects a monument as a reminder that the large stone will be "a witness against you" when the people inevitably fail to live up to their promise.

God the husband already knows the people will be unfaithful. And their subsequent history bears out Joshua's prediction. So we must ask the question: What kind of husband, in the face of serial infidelity, is willing to try again and again to woo the unfaithful spouse back into an intimate relationship? What kind of husband would show such patience and persistence? What kind of God would not give up on such people and walk away for good? What kind of God will never walk away from you and me? Jeremiah gives us the answer.

A Broken Kingdom and Broken Relationships

To get to Jeremiah, we have to fast forward four centuries from David's time. A lot has happened to the relationship between the people and God, and between the twelve original tribes. After the death of David's successor and son, Solomon, the kingdom intentionally broke apart—divided. Ten of the tribes became the Northern Kingdom of Israel, whose kings were not from the house of David. The two remaining tribes became the Southern Kingdom of Judah, which included Jerusalem.

Rulers in both kingdoms—which sometimes were allies and sometimes enemies—frequently "did what was evil in the sight of the Lord," as the chroniclers put it. By this, the chroniclers meant that kings and/or their wives worshipped foreign gods—a practice that began under Solomon—and encouraged the people to break the covenant in the same way. Most, according to the biblical writers, did evil. The worship of other gods continued for generations. When the kingdom divided, it left both the Northern and Southern kingdoms vulnerable to attack from foreign invaders.

The Northern Kingdom, Israel, was conquered by the Assyrian Empire (located in what today is northern Iraq) around 733 BCE, with most of its people being dispersed throughout the empire.

More than 100 years later, the Assyrian Empire gave way to the new regional power, Babylon, that invaded Judah in 609 BCE. The king of Judah paid tribute (or taxes) to Babylon to avoid destruction. Unwisely, his successor decided to discontinue the payments. This is where we meet Jeremiah.

A Human-Made Hell

Jeremiah is one of the best-known major prophets in the Hebrew Scriptures. His prophetic career spans some of the most critical events in the history of Judah—he warned of the impending conquest and saw the destruction of the Temple and his people taken into exile—and the book named for him spans fifty-two chapters. Jeremiah is often called the "weeping prophet" because of his wish that his eyes become "a fountain of tears" so that he might weep for the fate of the nation and the dead and dispersed among his people (9:1). His writings alternated between fulminations against how Judah's leaders and people had broken faith with God and lamentations over the destruction he foresaw. His warnings were unpopular, to say the least. At one point, the king ordered him confined in the bottom of a well, where he was left to die until a sympathetic guard freed him.

God chooses Jeremiah to speak to Judah on God's behalf, calling them to repentance:

> What wrong did your ancestors find in me
> > that they went far from me,
> and went after worthless things and became worthless themselves? . . .
> I brought you into a plentiful land
> > to eat its fruits and its good things.
> But when you entered you defiled my land
> > and made my heritage an abomination . . . .
>
> Has a nation changed its gods,
> > even though they are no gods? . . .
>
> You have prostituted yourself with many lovers,
> > and would you return to me?
> > > says the LORD.
>
> > > > (Jeremiah 2:5,7, 11; 3:1b)

Jeremiah warns Judah that if they do not return to God and placate the Babylonians—and if they do not stop worshipping idols, oppressing the poor, and shedding innocent blood—they will face the same fate as Israel. Babylon will destroy Jerusalem and send them into exile as well. But the people do not heed his warnings. Jeremiah also rails at perhaps the most grievous act of rebellion against God that the people of Judah ever committed. At a place called Topheth in the Valley of the Son of Hinnom, on the western and southwestern outskirts of ancient Jerusalem, the people go beyond the pale of idol worship and engage in child sacrifice. God accuses them of participating in the abominable act of burning children alive as an offering to Molech: "And they go on building the high place of Topheth, which is in the valley of the son of Hinnom, to burn their sons and their daughters in the fire—which I did not command, nor did it come into my mind" (Jeremiah 7:31).

If the people continued to turn their backs on God, warned Jeremiah, the Valley of Hinnom would become known as the Valley of Slaughter, and all of Jerusalem would become a waste (7:30-34).

> *Whenever you read the word hell in the Gospels, a footnote references Gehenna, the word Jesus uses to describe utter separation from God— a place created by humans, not by God.*

The Valley of Hinnom is also known by the name Gehinnom— or, as transliterated in Greek, the language of the New Testament, Gehenna. It is important to recognize how Gehenna was understood in Jeremiah and Jesus's time. After the abomination of child sacrifices ceased in Gehenna, by the time of Jesus it was a trash dump. Where children were once sacrificed by fire, there was now smoldering garbage with the poorest scavenging what others discarded. It was a place that was viewed with disgust. If you can't remember the word *Gehenna* being mentioned in the New Testament, that's because we don't see it in our English translations. Whenever you read the word *hell* in the Gospels, a footnote references Gehenna, the word Jesus uses to describe utter separation from God—a place created by humans, not by God.

Just as God could no more be present in the actions of people sacrificing their children to idols, when we walk away from God to pursue selfish interests and inflict pain on others, we create our own form of Gehenna. Haven't we all experienced moments that we would describe as a "living hell," whether they were induced by others or of our own making? I know I have. I create my own Gehenna when an action taken, or a harsh word spoken alienates me from those I love. When I break God's law of love. We see evidence of Gehennas in our communities and in our world lived out on our newsfeeds daily. I believe the warnings Jesus offers us about Gehenna are given so that we do not harm our life and health, our relationships with family and friends, or bring harm into the lives of others.

The Days Are Surely Coming

Jeremiah's oracles are full of the language of God "plucking up and breaking down" and "overthrowing and destroying." But Jeremiah is not just a prophet of doom and gloom. He also proclaims hope. In another performative act, just before the siege of Jerusalem begins, he buys a field in the countryside. Financially, the purchase makes no sense. The land is already under the occupation of the Babylonian invaders. But Jeremiah wants to make a point: The day will come, he says, when fields once again will be bought and sold in Judah, farmers will raise crops, and fortunes will be restored (Jeremiah 32:42-44). In other words, God will remember God's people.

In Jeremiah 31, one of the most powerfully moving passages in all of Scripture, Jeremiah makes the promise explicit. The destruction of the land is over. God will "sow the house of Israel and the house of Judah with the seed of humans and the seed of animals" (31:27). The people have broken faith, they have broken the covenant made through Moses, yet again, just as they did in the time of Moses, and just as David did despite God's blessings.

They have sunk to an unprecedented low point of depravity. They have taken the nation into a Gehenna of their own making.

In response, God does not declare the covenant null and void, as if it were a legal contract. Instead, God announces a new covenant—or, more appropriately stated, a renewed or reaffirmed covenant. In this renewal, God does not change the terms of the promise of faithful love for God's people; instead, God adopts a breathtaking new approach to how the covenant will be implemented and understood.

Bearing in mind just how utterly the people have broken faith with God, how completely they have estranged themselves from God's vision for the world, you may be able to reread Jeremiah's words with an even deeper appreciation of God's commitment to a relationship with rebellious human beings—with us:

> The days are surely coming, says the LORD, when I will make a new covenant with the house of Israel and the house of Judah. It will not be like the covenant that I made with their ancestors when I took them by the hand to bring them out of the land of Egypt—a covenant that they broke, though I was their husband, says the LORD. But this is the covenant that I will make with the house of Israel after those days, says the LORD: I will put my law within them, and I will write it on their hearts; and I will be their God, and they shall be my people. No longer shall they teach one another or say to each other, "Know the LORD," for they shall all know me, from the least of them to the greatest, says the LORD; for I will forgive their iniquity, and remember their sin no more.
>
> (Jeremiah 31:31-34)

This covenant will not be written on stone tablets as in the days of Moses; instead, God's Law will reside within them, written by God's merciful hand on their hearts, on our hearts. The days are surely coming....Jeremiah's words offered great hope for the people of Judah during their approximately seventy long years of exile in Babylon. As they dreamed of returning to their homes; of replanting their vineyards; of rebuilding the Temple and worshipping again in Jerusalem, they remembered God's promise: The days are surely coming.... The day is surely coming. The time *is* coming when God, remembering God's people, will take their hearts and, line by line, write the law of the love of God and neighbor within them—within us. They, and we, will intimately know God, our husband, and he will remember only how much he loves his bride. The covenant will be renewed. The past, the infidelity, the faithlessness—all will be forgotten entirely.

Jeremiah's words offer a great deal of hope for us today, especially during the season of Lent. How does God propose to write on our stone-cold hearts? How will God enable us to do what we have never been able to do on our own? Let's face it. We still have a propensity to think that we know better than God at times—or at least we fail to consider what God might want of us. Like the Israelites, we have a bent toward wandering, toward making gods out of all sorts of things that aren't gods: like our careers, our wealth and status, our homes, cars, wardrobes, political parties, and leaders. The list is endless.

We forget that we, like Abraham, are blessed to be a blessing to others. We build our own Gehennas. We find ourselves driven into self-imposed exiles by our self-centered nature, living out the consequences of separating ourselves from the one source of infinite love and peace; wondering why our lives feel empty or futile. We may, on occasion, walk away and forget about God, but God remembers us. Always.

Our human propensity—yours and mine—to wander and forget, reminds me of my favorite lines from the old hymn, "Come Thou Fount of Every Blessing":

> O to grace how great a debtor
> daily I'm constrained to be!
> Let Thy goodness like a fetter,
> bind my wandering heart to thee.

> Prone to wander, Lord, I feel it,
> prone to leave the God I love;
> here's my heart, O take and seal it,
> seal it for thy courts above.[1]

Here's my heart, Lord. Take it. Bind it. Write your law of love on it. Let me know you in such a way that I can be faithful to your covenant; that your love becomes my love; and that my love becomes a reflection of yours to everyone I encounter. That is my prayer during Lent. What if that was our prayer as both individuals and communities of faith? How different would our communities and our world look if we took this prayer to heart each day? History demonstrates our repeated failure to curb our bent toward wandering, self-centeredness, corruption, stony hearts, or violence. But God's grace has the ability to reach into our hearts and change us.

As we have seen through this biblical arc of salvation that is our story, in the face of humanity's forgetfulness and faithlessness, God faithfully continues to remember—to reach out to renew the salvific and life-giving covenants made with Noah, Abraham, Moses, and David. Time after time, God persists in trying to woo God's children toward God's love and goodness. God persists in inviting you and me to live in that grace, for God knows that only there can our hearts find true fulfillment and peace. As St. Augustine writes in his *Confessions*, "You have made us for yourself, O Lord, and our hearts are restless until they find their rest in you."[2]

Through Jesus, God continues to renew the covenants. Jesus is a son of Abraham, a descendant of David. He is the promised Davidic king who, as the Word made flesh, restores God as ruler, not just of Israel but of all humanity. In renewing the covenant made with Moses, Jesus becomes the new Moses and initiates the new covenant that Jeremiah announced.

Jesus Initiates the New Covenant

Jeremiah is the only Hebrew Scripture that mentions a "new covenant," though Isaiah and Ezekiel use the same imagery as Jeremiah (Isaiah 59:21; Ezekiel 11:19-20; 37:24-28). According to Luke's Gospel, Jesus also references a "new covenant" the night before his crucifixion. It's the only Gospel that uses this term first applied by Jeremiah. (You may also find "new covenant" in Matthew, but some of the oldest manuscripts simply say "covenant," as Mark does; John does not use this term at all.)

We can see that the spirit of Jeremiah's words is present throughout Jesus's teachings. In the Sermon on the Mount, Jesus reinterprets the law of Moses to focus less on the words inscribed on tablets than on what is in the heart. In his litany that repeats the familiar words, "You have heard it said.... But I say to you," Jesus references the letter of the Law and then directs his listeners toward the spirit of the Law, the heart of the Law.

The Law forbids murder, but Jesus teaches that anyone who holds anger and hatred in their heart has violated the spirit of the Law just as surely as a killer (Matthew 5:22). The Law forbids adultery, but Jesus says those who lust after someone else have already committed adultery in their hearts (Matthew 5:28). The Law forbids evil actions, but Jesus teaches that evil thoughts that ignite those actions arise from the heart (Matthew 15:19). Jesus reminds his listeners that the "pure in heart" will see God (Matthew 5:8) and that that "where your treasure is, there your heart will be also" (Matthew 6:21).

> *Our hearts—need to be inscribed with Jesus's interpretation of the Law.*

People's hearts—our hearts—need to be inscribed with Jesus's interpretation of the Law, and Jesus has come to do just that. He has come, as he declares, not to abolish the Law but to fulfill it. In human form and flesh, God has arrived to usher in Jeremiah's new covenant—the covenant of the heart. In Jesus, the days that were surely coming have arrived.

Yet it is in John's Gospel that we can clearly see what it looks like when God inscribes the covenant on human hearts.

According to John (and only John), as Jesus and the disciples sit down to dinner for the final time, it is evident that no one has washed their grimy, road-weary feet. This was a job typically performed by a servant, and jars of water were kept near the door for this purpose. Were the disciples afraid that if one of them began washing his feet, the others would expect him to continue with theirs? We don't know, but no one moved to make the offer.

So, in the middle of the meal, Jesus rises from the table, takes off his outer robe, and ties a towel around his waist. Assuming the dress and demeanor of a slave, he takes a basin of water, gets down on bended knee, and moves from one pair of dirty feet to the next, twenty-four dirty feet in all, washing them and drying them with the towel. Peter, horrified, vehemently objects and is embarrassed that the Lord is doing this to him, but eventually consents to Jesus's gracious overture of servanthood. Even Judas, who will betray Jesus before the night ends, has his feet lovingly washed. What we learn, is that Jesus's washing of the disciples' feet is not about dirty feet. It is symbolic of something much greater.

The gathering, for which Jesus sets the tone by serving the disciples, is a moving picture of that kind of intimacy I described at the beginning of this chapter—the intimacy we need and long for. Imagine how the disciples must have remembered that evening years later. They were the last people to share a meal around a table with Jesus before his arrest and crucifixion. They remembered that he announced that they should no longer be considered his servants but as his friends—people he loves and trusts deeply. They remembered that he told them he would not leave them orphaned, in spite of what was about to happen—that the Spirit (or the Advocate) would come and dwell in them, not unlike a covenant that was inscribed on their inmost selves. They remembered he told them that he said he had overcome the world—and had called them "out of the world" along with him.

Most of all, they remembered that Jesus had given them a calling as part of this covenant—a call to love completely and fearlessly. As he explained to his astonished disciples, with the once pristine towel now damp and covered in the grime of the disciples' feet, and after Jesus had put his robe back on: "Do you know what I have done to you? You call me Teacher and Lord, and you are right, for that is what I am. So if I, your Lord and Teacher, have washed your feet, you also ought to wash one another's feet. For I have set you an example, that you should also do as I have done to you.... I give you a new commandment, that you love one another. Just as I have loved you, you also should love one another. By this everyone will know that you are my disciples, if you have love for one another" (from John 13:1-15, 34-35).

> *We exclaim we are Jesus's disciples, not in the way that we admonish one other, try to prove one another wrong, or exclude one another, but in the way we love.*

Everyone will know that we are Jesus's disciples in the way that we love one another. In the way we feed the hungry, bind the wounds of those who are hurting, visit the lonely and the imprisoned, show kindness to a stranger, offer forgiveness to one another. We exclaim we are Jesus's disciples, not in the way that we admonish one other, try to prove one another wrong, or exclude one another, but in the way we love.

But we already know from Jesus's earlier words in the Gospels, that this is hardly a new commandment. It is a commandment directly from Torah (Leviticus 19:18). In conveying the imperative to love, the author of 1 John explains: "I am writing you no new commandment but an old commandment that you have had from the beginning" (2:7).

Just as Jesus, in telling the parable of the good Samaritan, interpreted for the teacher of the law what it meant to be a neighbor, Jesus demonstrates to his disciples the kind of love that will define them as faithful followers—a love that is willing to humble itself and become a servant. Tomorrow, he will trade his basin and towel for a cross, and they (and we) will see the depth of what the new/old commandment entails. The commandment to love is not new. What is new is the revelation of the depth of love involved in following Jesus all the way to the cross, and the power of divine love to bring resurrection to our lives and the way we love.

Just as Jesus showed the disciples an example on their last night together of what self-giving love looked like in practice, he showed them the next day what he meant when he said, "No one has greater love than this, to lay down one's life for one's friends" (John 15:13). And just as they were shocked that the one they called "Master" would wash their feet like a lowly servant, they were horrified that the one they believed to be the Messiah could suffer a horrible, humiliating, torturous death like a criminal. As they surely recalled Jesus's words from the night before, they may have begun to fathom the depth of Jesus's love for them.

When we encounter the risen Jesus, may we, as his followers did, come to appreciate both the price of love and the power of love to cast away fear and liberate us. In the flush of Jesus's love, now part and parcel of who they are, the disciples, and we, have been freed. Through the Spirit, with the law of love inscribed on our hearts, we are now able, as Jeremiah's new covenant proclaimed, to truly know God. By following the commandment to "love to the end" (John 13:1), the disciples embraced a new relationship with Jesus, not as servants but as friends. An intimate friendship we are invited to enter into. Their witness inspires us to live by the way of love—and to love fully and fearlessly, secure in the understanding that we don't have to surrender to the world's self-centric standards. Like Jesus, we can overcome the world. We can incorporate into our being the love that costs all we have but sets us free to live in an intimate relationship with our Creator. We can claim the power, as John's Gospel put it, to be even more than children beloved by God—we can become *of* God.

CHAPTER SIX

Jesus and the New Covenant

[Jesus] said to them, "I have eagerly desired to eat this Passover with you before I suffer, for I tell you, I will not eat it until it is fulfilled in the kingdom of God." Then he took a cup, and after giving thanks he said, "Take this and divide it among yourselves, for I tell you that from now on I will not drink of the fruit of the vine until the kingdom of God comes." Then he took a loaf of bread, and when he had given thanks he broke it and gave it to them, saying, "This is my body, which is given for you. Do this in remembrance of me." And he did the same with the cup after supper, saying, "This cup that is poured out for you is the new covenant in my blood."

(Luke 22:15-20)

I received from the Lord what I also handed on to you, that the Lord Jesus on the night when he was betrayed took a loaf of bread, and when he had given thanks, he broke it and said, "This is my body that is [broken] for you.[1] Do this in remembrance of me." In the same way he took the cup also, after supper, saying, "This cup is the new covenant in my blood. Do this, as often as you drink it, in remembrance of me." For as often as you eat this bread and drink the cup, you proclaim the Lord's death until he comes.

(1 Corinthians 11:23-26)

From the time of Adam and Eve, God's children have walked away from and "forgotten" the One who never forgets them, who always remembers them, just as I did in my twenties. As we have seen, turning away inevitably produced (and still produces) disastrous results in the form of violence, evil, immorality, injustice, oppression of others, or just a feeling of emptiness. God continued to find new ways to remind God's beloved creation of the deep love God held for them, and how they might return and live in the way God intended, a way that would be best for all humanity, to live together in that love.

I don't know if you experience this kind of frustration in your homes with technology, but it seems that, almost weekly, something in our home malfunctions. The television that worked perfectly last night offers only a blank screen when we hit the green "on" button on the remote control. The face of my phone freezes. My computer offers a multicolored circle that continues to spin while not allowing me to access or edit any documents (I call it the spinning circle of death). We have all discovered that when things stop working, sometimes the best solution is to "reboot"—to unplug for a while, plug back in, and start over.

> *Sometimes we need to unplug—stop and assess what is going wrong in our life and in our relationship with others and with God—and plug back in.*

It appears the same is true for people. Sometimes we need to unplug—stop and assess what is going wrong in our life and in our relationship with others and with God—and plug back in. God keeps trying to provide new ways to show the character of God, who God is, and how much we are loved. Starting with Noah and Abraham, each successive covenant instituted by God is a sort of reboot to try and produce the same result; people who work as they should, love as God intends, and enjoy the "abundant life" that Jesus said he came to model for, and offer to, us all.

Jesus, as the new covenant, offers us, yet again, an opportunity to reboot our relationship with God through him. Jesus institutes a new covenant shrouded in memory, and as such, we are called to remember what God has done for us through each of these covenants. So, in this final chapter of our Lenten journey, you are invited to remember those covenants, remember why God came in human form to make a new covenant with us. We will explore the importance and power of Jesus's table ministry. This is the place from which the new covenant is inaugurated, and we will see how Jesus, the new covenant, leads us to the home, the land that he will show us, through the cross. He gives us a new identity in him, one that empowers us, through the Holy Spirit, to live out his calling on our lives both individually and as a community of the covenant.

Remembering the Previous Covenants

God always asks people to remember what God has done for them in each covenant, and Jesus does the same as he institutes the new covenant.

So, I invite you to go back and reread God's second reboot in the making of the covenant with Abraham (Genesis 12:1-4; 17:1-10) in order to understand how it relates to the others and to Jesus's covenant. Within the story we find a formula that we will see repeated later. There is a call to follow God or walk in the way of God. God spells out what God has done or will do for the person who is receiving news of the covenant (God remembers Abraham). There is a change in name or identity that prepares him for the changed life ahead (Abram, exalted father, becomes Abraham, father of multitudes).

A reboot of the covenant with Abraham comes through Moses and David. We see that Abraham's descendants do become a great nation. The people *do* receive land, a place to call home, a place to live and grow. Kings *are* born through Abraham and Sarah. The people *do* become as numerous as the sand and stars, just as God promised. We see glimmers of hope that humanity might follow God's ways and be a light to the nations that would draw all people to love God and one another.

Yet time and again, we as God's people "forget." Whether intentionally or not, we stop following and strike out on our own self-destructive paths. We create idols that replace God in our lives. We covet others' possessions, jobs, positions, power, and influence, thinking that if only we could have those things, our lives would be better, more satisfying. Our hearts would be full. Our spirits would soar. Yet if we attain those things, while setting God aside, our lives can still feel hollow. That's because we lost, or forgot, our identity as children of God somewhere along the way. We put other things ahead of God, just like all those earlier covenant breakers.

In response, God never gives up on us, never forgets. Instead, God continues to pursue us, to reach out in love. And in the coming of Jesus, God provides a dramatic, paradigm-shifting covenant reboot, becoming one of us, experiencing human emotion, human pain, and human death.

One of Us

Years ago, the late radio host Paul Harvey recounted a parable about a man who had difficulty understanding and believing in the concept of the Incarnation, or God coming to us in the flesh of Jesus. One evening the man was alone in his home as a snowstorm blew in. Within moments he began to hear a thudding sound at the window. When he investigated, he discovered a flock of birds, trapped in the storm, trying to fly through his window to take shelter from the storm. Wanting to keep the flock from freezing, he desperately tried to coax them into his nearby barn, but neither leaving a trail of breadcrumbs nor trying to shoo them into the shelter proved helpful.

The man realized that the birds were terrified of him. They didn't know that he was trying to help them. The man thought to himself, "If only I could be a bird . . . and speak their language. Then I could tell them not to be afraid. Then I could show them the way to the safe, warm barn. But I would have to be one of them so they could see . . . and hear . . . and understand." And in that moment, he heard church bells pealing in the distance, and he sank to his knees in the snow.[2] In that moment, the man understood what God was trying to do through Jesus.

As we consider God's plan to offer a new covenant, a reboot of the former covenants, we, too, need to remember God's desire to become one of us so we can see . . . and hear . . . and understand more completely—more intimately—God's deepest love and desires for us.

Remembering the Importance and Power of the Table

Most of my favorite childhood memories center around holiday dinners. I come from a very large extended family with more aunts, uncles, and cousins than you could count! During most holidays the entire family would gather at our home because we lived in the country and had space outdoors to set up tables to accommodate everyone.

Growing up in a large family offers an opportunity to experience a microcosm of society. We were rich/poor, young/ old, Catholic/Protestant, blue collar and white. Straight as an arrow, and released straight from prison. Yet all were welcome at my mom's table. *Everyone.* Including friends from college who had no place to go. If someone asked Mom, "You're not going to invite *her*, are you?" (because in a big family someone is always angry with someone else), Mom would say, "Of course! It's family. Everyone's invited."

Many holidays, we would have seventy or eighty for dinner, but everyone brought something to share. There was always an abundance of food; If you were hungry for it, it was on Mom's table. Everyone was invited, and no one left hungry.

Jesus's table was the same. In the Bible, banquets and dinners often represent invitations to the kingdom of God. Most often, Jesus is seen eating with tax collectors and sinners, those who occupy the lowest rungs of society, but he also includes those on the highest. Everyone is invited to dine with Jesus. And Jesus's disciples, often present at his open table, would have witnessed the countless times he blessed and broke bread before distributing it to his table guests.

After Jesus miraculously feeds 5,000 people with the five loaves and two fish shared by a young boy, the crowd follows him, wanting him to keep producing bread for them. They have been fed, but they are not satisfied. And Jesus tells them, "Do not work for the food that perishes but for the food that endures for eternal life" (John 6:27). The crowds were filled with their expectations for Jesus—that he would be a king to keep their bellies full, a genie granting their every wish—and he essentially says to them, You don't get it, "I am the bread of life. Whoever comes to me will never be hungry, and whoever believes in me will never be thirsty" (John 6:35).

Jesus reminds us that there is a hunger and a longing in us—in our hearts—that only the Bread of Life can satisfy. Jesus cares about the condition of our hearts. After all, as Jeremiah envisioned, it is the vessel upon which the new covenant will be inscribed. With the coming of the Word made flesh, our hearts have the capacity to become pliable and ready to receive what God through Jesus Christ has prepared for us. So, the question is: What are you hungry for? For what does your heart yearn?

> *What are you hungry for?*
> *For what does your heart yearn?*

If we are honest with ourselves, all of us are hungry for unconditional love and acceptance, for peace to rule our hearts and our
world instead of fear and anxiety, and for joy and true fulfillment.
Some of us are hungry for compassion. Some of us are hungry for
forgiveness for a past wrong, or the ability to forgive someone who
has wronged us. In trying to calm our restless hearts, at times we
seek to fill the void with bread that doesn't satisfy. We hope the
next wardrobe purchase, job, spouse, school, promotion, title,
drink, or politician will fill our hungry heart; but we receive it
and find ourselves empty again. We need the Bread of Life who
came that we might, as he said, "have life and have it abundantly"
(John 10:10), who came to shape our hearts to be humble like his
(Matthew 11:29). We need the one who invites us to eat and drink
of the new covenant.

The New Covenant Begins at the Table

The days we call Holy Week had been busy and emotionally
charged for Jesus and his followers. The Scriptures tell us that, in
the days leading up to that fateful week, Jesus "set his face to go
to Jerusalem" (Luke 9:51). He travels on Palm Sunday with his
disciples and crowds of followers to celebrate the Passover, but
there is also an air of determination and purpose in all that Jesus
does, beginning with his triumphal ride into the city mounted on
a donkey—a prophetic act that announced he was the coming
Messiah (Zechariah 9:9).

This determination continued throughout the week with the
dramatic cleansing of the Temple, and through Jesus's recognition
of the lavish anointing of his head with costly ointment as a

Remember

foreshadowing of his death and burial. Now, Jesus gathers his disciples together on Thursday to share what will be their last meal together before his death. It will be a meal that names and inaugurates the new covenant, a covenant for all. And yet, this covenant is not wholly new. In a sacrificially significant way, it shows more fully the love God has always had for God's children, and God's desire for them to remain in relationship—at the table, if you will—with their Creator.

The Gospel writers of Matthew, Mark, and Luke all record similar actions and statements by Jesus the night before he went to the cross. Luke makes it clear that he and his disciples gather to commemorate Passover with a holy meal that had been celebrated by Jews for centuries, recounting God's mighty acts in delivering the people of Israel from slavery in Egypt.

As Jesus sits at the table and blesses and breaks unleavened bread, his disciples might have been surprised, or at least confused, to hear these words: "This is my body that is broken for you." The bread that normally would have been eaten to remember the haste with which the Israelites fled Egypt (there was no time to allow the bread to rise before their departure), will now become a remembrance of Jesus's body that would be broken on the cross the next day. And even though Jesus has warned them of his impending death, the disciples have not seriously considered this reality. They are still hoping that Jesus will become the militaristic, Davidic king that will rule over Israel and displace the Roman occupation. As of yet, they do not understand that this Davidic king's kingdom is not of this world.

After Jesus blesses, breaks, and shares the bread of his body with those gathered at his table, he lifts a cup of wine.

Throughout a traditional Passover meal, or Seder (meaning "order"), participants consume four cups of wine. The third cup, drunk toward the end of the meal, is known as "the cup of redemption," symbolizing the Israelites' physical redemption from

Egypt. We don't know all of the components present during the Passover meal of Jesus's day, but it may have been this cup that Jesus blessed, saying, "Drink from it, all of you, for this is my blood of the [new] covenant, which is poured out for many for the forgiveness of sins" (Matthew 26:27-28).[3] The cup that once remembered the blood of the Passover lambs, delivering the firstborn Hebrews from death, now becomes the blood of Christ, God incarnate, poured out in love to overcome our slavery to sin and death.

While we don't know for certain if it was Jesus's intention to connect his words regarding the new covenant in his blood to Jeremiah's, for he doesn't speak of the law written on hearts during this meal, the listeners and readers of his words who were steeped in Hebrew Scripture would have made that connection, for they had been waiting for the day that was "surely coming" when God would enact a new covenant written not on tablets of stone, but on the hearts of God's people. Jesus was well aware of the people's waiting for that day. Therefore, I believe that Jesus meant to make this connection between his words at the table and Jeremiah's prophecy.

> *Jesus wasn't beginning a new tradition. He was revealing in a new way the message God had been conveying to God's people for centuries.*

The actual genesis of the church's ritual of sharing in the Lord's Supper, or Communion, did not begin with what we now call the Last Supper. It was set thousands of years before through the rituals of the Passover meal. Jesus wasn't beginning a new tradition. He was revealing in a new way the message God had been conveying to God's people for centuries. God loves us enough to save us, to

Remember

deliver us from all of the things that enslave us—again, and again, and again. God loves us with an everlasting love and faithfulness that will never allow God to forget us. This is why Jesus told his disciples that, when you observe this meal—when you break this bread, and drink this cup—"do this in remembrance of me" (Luke 22:19).

Mark, almost certainly the first Gospel to be written (and a source for Matthew and Luke), does not describe the covenant sealed with Jesus's blood as "new." However, Paul's account of Jesus's words at the table (1 Corinthians 11:23-26) that were passed on to him, and are included in the opening page of this chapter, do include "new covenant." Since Paul wrote his letters several years before Mark's Gospel, it is safe to assume that the early church understood these as Jesus's words even before the Gospels were penned. However, Mark places emphasis on another point. In Mark's account of the Last Supper, Jesus tells his disciples: "This is my blood of the covenant, which is poured out for many" (Mark 14:24).

As devout Jews, the disciples would have understood that earlier covenants were ratified with blood. In ritualizing the covenant between God and the Israelites, Moses sprinkles blood on the people to make them parties to the agreement (Exodus 24:8). As mentioned in chapter 2, Genesis 15 describes a formal ceremony, involving the death of animals, by which the covenant was ratified between God and Abraham. Cutting the animals in half symbolized how the two parties pledged their lives to keep the covenant. Notably, only God passed between the two pieces of the slaughtered animal, as the ritual required. Abraham was invited to walk in faith, but only God was obligated to keep the promise.

As Mark presents it to us, just as Jesus gave people a new, liberating way of understanding the Law, he reaffirms the old covenant with God's people in a powerful and startling new way. Here, the blood being shed is not that of an animal but of the

106

Word made flesh. In effect, Jesus is saying, "I am delivering on my unbreakable promise of love to you through the outpouring of my own life's blood." From Mark, we may understand what happened as less of a new covenant than as a renewal of God's unilateral promise of love offered to all people.

The new covenant, instituted at the table, was the beginning of a new life, a new direction, and a new identity for the disciples, for the church, and for us.

The Cross Is Not the End

Christians have long interpreted Jesus's death as the cancellation for all time of humanity's debt to sin. But we also know from this story that we have now followed, beginning with Noah and Abraham, that God makes a habit of setting our unpaid debts aside. Over and over, God reboots the covenant after humans break the bond of trust and choose their own path instead of following God's.

Only, now, God reaffirms this covenant not with words but, through Jesus, with God's own suffering flesh and spilled blood.

The cross is a place of pain and desolation that feels far from God. Like the Valley of Hinnom where children were sacrificed during Jeremiah's time, it represents the extreme of human rebellion against God's kingdom of love. Jesus felt that physical and emotional pain directly, expressing it from the cross in the words of the psalmist, "My God, my God, why have you forsaken me?" (Matthew 27:46). Jesus experienced, as the Israelites did, and as we do, the all-too-human *feeling* of being forsaken by God, and yet he knew, and clung to hope in, the end of the Psalm 22 that he quoted from the cross.

If he had the strength to complete the words of this song he had learned from his youth, others standing near the cross might have heard these words, "He did not hide his face from me, but heard when I cried to him.... Before him [the LORD] shall bow all who go down to the dust, and I shall live for him...future generations will be told about the LORD and proclaim his deliverance to a people yet unborn, saying that he has done it" (from Psalm 22:24b, 29-31). These words Jesus quotes from the cross are not words of defeat but of victory. So, for those who accept Jesus's invitation to "take up your cross and follow me," the barren, fearful hill of Golgotha is only a way station. The old hymn had it right: For you and me, "the way of the cross leads home."

> ## *The cross takes us to our true home, which is not of this world.*

The cross takes us to our true home, which is not of this world (whether we are living in this world or in the life to come). It can often be a difficult journey. Even Jesus asked that, if it were possible, he be spared this cup of suffering. Traveling the way of the cross requires letting go *of* ourselves, dying *to* ourselves, and trusting. But it is how we come face-to-face with God.

When we come to the cross, where Jesus invites us to follow, we confront our own habitual brokenness. If we are honest, we see more than just the Roman soldiers who carried out the Crucifixion, the misguided religious authorities who pushed the fearful governor into ordering it, the two bandits hanging by Jesus's side, and the innocent women who witnessed and wept. If we are honest, we see ourselves. We confront our own betrayal of Jesus, our own rebellion against God's covenants—our repeated failure to love our neighbor. We confront humanity's unbroken record of broken trust. We realize that we have taken ourselves to Gehenna, a place as barren and frightening as Golgotha. We may weep bitter tears, as Peter wept, over our faithlessness that mocks our professions of undying faith.

But we also can weep tears of joy and amazement when we contemplate God's response to our brokenness. We marvel at what God has done through Jesus, enduring one of the worst forms of human death, to show us the way that leads beyond death, beyond fear, and beyond hurt and pain.

What if, instead of thinking of Jesus's death as a blood sacrifice demanded by a wrathful God, we understood it as the way Jesus has shown us on our journey toward our home with the God who has always loved us with an unfathomable, eternal love? What if, instead of interpreting the cross purely as the ultimate act of atonement for human sin, we recognized it primarily as the ultimate act of love by a God who will not give up on us?

Jesus knows that his cross is not the end. He knows that the cross, lifted to the sky, will someday become a sign to us of the new covenant (much like the rainbow was for Noah). He knows that, through the cross, he will become the fulfillment of all of the covenants. But we don't yet know any of this—not until he shows us through his resurrection. Only with the shocking joy of Easter did the disciples begin to comprehend what Jesus meant on his last night with them when he said: "This is my blood of the new covenant." Only in the joy of the Resurrection did they understand his words, "In the world you face persecution, but take courage: I have conquered the world!" (John 16:33).

Writing on Our Hearts

Having followed Jesus to the cross and come face-to-face with the risen Christ, we might ask, "How?" How does he write the law on our hearts? How is it that, when confronted with human suffering, our hearts immediately tell us that we should do something to help? By the same token, how is it that, immediately after we say an unkind word to someone, betray a confidence, or break a promise, we feel a pang of guilt in our hearts? How is it that, when confronted with an emptiness in my heart and soul while sitting on a congested Dallas freeway, I instinctively knew the cause of that emptiness? The biblical answer to these questions is that this is the work of the Holy Spirit that both writes the law on our hearts and reminds us of that law when we have memory lapses (John 14:26).

However, Jeremiah's prophecy regarding the new covenant seems rather utopian in nature, doesn't it? For we all know that, even with the law written on our hearts, we still forget about God. We don't know God as fully as we should or would like. There are still division, war, hunger, injustice, and violence in the world. And we definitely still need to teach one another. We are all too human, but the Holy Spirit is working within us; calling us, teaching us, leading us to where God would have us go. We are human, and thankfully, God is eternally gracious.

The Holy Spirit is *already* among us planting seeds of Christ's kingdom, while we live in hope and pray for the *not yet*—for the new thing that God is doing among us in Jesus Christ and for the fulfillment of his kingdom on earth as it is in heaven—as Christ continues his work within us through the power of his Spirit.

Sometimes the Spirit comes to us like a wild wind or a raging fire (as it did in Acts 2), and sometimes God's Spirit comes to us as gently as a quiet breath (John 20:22), or a cool drink of water (John 4:14; 7:37-39). May we, this Lenten season, attune ourselves to that writing on our hearts so that we may recognize and respond to the wind, fire, gentle breath, or water when they appear.

In Remembrance of Me

I love cleaning up after a dinner spent with family, especially one that includes a member we haven't seen in almost a year. Such was the case a few months ago. The evening was one of those rare gems that was inexplicably glorious. After everyone had left for the evening, as I was washing each glass and collecting place mats and napkins from in front of each chair at the table, I pictured the faces of those gathered, and the exact spot where each family member sat. I remembered their contributions to the stories, the laughter, and the unspoken love that permeated the room. That evening I thought, "Jesus knew what he was doing when he gathered people to sit down with him for a meal." These moments can become moments of pure grace and joy—dare I say—sacred moments? It certainly was for me on that night.

I wondered if the disciples remembered with the same fondness I did that evening all of the times they gathered for meals with Jesus—the stories, laughter, and joy they shared. I think they must have, for some of them are recorded for us, down to the detail of where the beloved disciple sat the night Jesus washed their feet at the dinner table and offered them a new commandment (John 13:23). The stories we have of Jesus sharing his final meal with his disciples are really ones where Jesus asks them (and us) to remember—as if they could ever forget—each time they gather to eat and drink, the significance and symbolism of the bread and wine that they share.

I wonder if they realized early on how sacred that moment would become for them, or if it took some time for the moment to fully register. My guess is that they had no idea that the words Jesus spoke to their intimate circle on that dark night would continue to be read, chanted, sung, and prayed by more than two billion followers around the globe 2,000 years later. They probably couldn't imagine that the love that permeated the room that night would still permeate the lives and hearts of followers today—a love that has been reaching out to us since the beginning of Creation. And it does so because the Word made flesh invites us to sit at the table with him and partake of the new covenant.

We discussed earlier that remembering is vital to our knowing God's salvation and redemption. Out of compassion and love God "remembers" God's people and covenants are made, and from that remembering God offers deliverance, redemption, mercy, and salvation. In return, we, as God's people, are called to celebrate and remember God's mighty acts effected on our behalf. Remembering makes us better people. Remembering rekindles our love of God and each other, much like the way retelling stories of how you met your spouse, why you fell in love, and the struggles you've endured together keeps the embers of love aglow in your relationship.

> **Remembering is vital to our knowing God's salvation and redemption.**

Participating in the liturgy and sacrament of Holy Communion, sitting at Christ's table, I believe, is one of the chief means of keeping our love for God and love for our neighbors alive and well, because it calls us to remember God's love for us; particularly the part of the liturgy known as The Great Thanksgiving. During The Great Thanksgiving we offer praise to God for all of God's mighty acts offered on our behalf. During Lent we remember,

> You [God] formed us into your image
> and breathed into us the breath of life.
> When we turned away, and our love failed, your love
> remained steadfast.
> When rain fell upon the earth for forty days...
> you bore up the ark... [and] saved Noah and his family....
> When you led your people to Mount Sinai...
> you gave us your commandments and made us your
> covenant people.[4]

God made covenants with Noah and Moses, but God also made *us*, through those actions, through Christ's sacrifice for us,

God's covenant people. These were not actions taken by God in the ancient past solely to benefit an ancient people, but for *all* of God's people—for you and me and for future generations. The Great Thanksgiving continues by describing Jesus's actions in the world and words he spoke at the table:

> "Take, eat; this is my body which is given for you.
> Do this in remembrance of me....
> Drink from this all of you; this is my blood of the new
> covenant....
> Do this as often as you drink it, in remembrance of me."

The minister, upon finishing these words, lifts her hands in the air speaking to God,

> And so, in remembrance of these your mighty acts in
> Jesus Christ,
> we offer ourselves in praise and thanksgiving,
> as a holy and living sacrifice, in union with Christ's
> offering for us...[5]

In remembrance of all that God has done for us, we offer ourselves. Knowing what God has done for us, how can we *not* offer ourselves? How can we help but offer ourselves as a holy and living sacrifice as we remember the God who remembers us?

Community of the Covenant

As you can tell, I love celebrating Communion, remembering Jesus's sacrifice made on our behalf. Although I almost always sense Christ's presence at his table, there have been two times in my life when I have been unexpectedly surprised and shocked by that presence. In the first, I experienced my call to ministry while helping serve Communion at a retreat. Holding a chalice and repeatedly offering the cup to participants, I sensed God saying, "*This* is what you should be doing." The second happened several summers ago traveling with a group in Greece. We made a stop on the Island of Patmos, where St. John was exiled during the persecution of Christians late in the first century.

Patmos is not very beautiful. It looks like a place to which you would be exiled! It is small, scrubby, dry; and high in the hills, there is a small cave where it is said that John lived and received from God a vision. The vision was not meant to frighten us, as some would interpret it, but to bring comfort and hope for those who were hungry for relief and release from persecution and oppression. This vision we know as Revelation.

My expectations were low for this pilgrimage. I assumed there would be throngs of people and lots of cheap St. John trinkets being sold, and there were. But what I hadn't expected was immediately adjacent to this unimposing cave: a tiny chapel, connected directly to the cave so that we tourists, sitting contemplating the sights in the cave, could also look across on this Sunday morning to see and hear a Greek Orthodox priest chanting the liturgy of a Communion service, in Greek, to Greek worshippers.

There was the tourist side—the "cave" side—and the Greek Orthodox worshipping community "chapel" side. We tourists respectfully stayed on our side. As the priest continued his musical chanting, I was able to comprehend bits of the Greek liturgy from my seminary days and its words repeatedly washed over me: *Kyrie Eleison, Christe Eleison* (Lord have mercy, Christ have mercy). In that moment I was unexpectedly overwhelmed by the sense of Christ's presence. I began weeping at the thought that, on this small island if not in this very place, John received an incredible vision from Christ 2,000 years ago that still speaks comfort and hope to us today.

In the vision, those saints who had been persecuted were singing and worshipping Christ day and night. As I looked across at the Communion table, with the priest's chanting ringing in my ears, I couldn't help but sense the presence of all the saints who have gone before, singing praises to God. And though our ordeals may not compare with theirs, I also thought of those in this day, and in my own congregation, going through ordeals of abuse and oppression, of family and relational problems, of tragic loss and grief, and discrimination, and wishing they could hear John's words in Revelation addressed to these saints and to us: "Blessed are those who are invited to the marriage supper of the Lamb.... They will hunger no more and thirst no more" (Revelation 19:9; 7:16).

As the priest repeatedly sang the words *Soma tou Christou*— the body of Christ—while pressing bread into the open hands of the worshipping crowd on the chapel side of John's former home, a young teenage boy, clearly on the tourist side of the cave, physically expressed what most of us were hungry to do. He spontaneously jumped up, ran across the open space between cave and chapel, saying, "I want some! I want some!" We tourists held our breath waiting to see what would happen, and then... the priest smiled, lifted a piece of bread, and gently pressed it into this young foreigner-become-family member's hand, welcoming him to Christ's table to receive the Bread of Life.

My mother is long deceased, but today, whenever we have a holiday meal and serve Mom's turkey and cornbread dressing, memories come flooding back of those times around her table. It is as if we are surrounded by all of our big, diverse family once again. I understand that what made those times special wasn't about the food. It was about finding a place of belonging, a home. It was about finding unconditional love and acceptance—sometimes finding an aunt or uncle who would offer guidance and advice whether you asked for it or not! It was about relationships. It was about family. We came hungry to experience something more than the fleeting fullness of the meal. We came hungry for the lasting taste and fullness of love and acceptance.

Christ's table, and his words declaring the new covenant, remind us that as brothers and sisters adopted into God's covenantal family and invited to Christ's banquet, we're stuck with each other; we're family. All of God's covenants, and Christ's table especially, teach us that faith isn't about being right or perfect or always being in agreement. It is about feeding and being fed. It's about the unconditional love of God that keeps reaching out to us, calling us to a better and more abundant life. It's about offering ourselves as a holy and living sacrifice in union with Christ's offering for us from the cross. It's about remembering the God who remembers us, and remembering those whom God remembers.

What Wondrous Love Is This

One of my favorite hymns, traditionally sung during Holy Week, begins with the words:

> What wondrous love is this, O my soul, O my soul,
>   what wondrous love is this, O my soul!
> What wondrous love is this that caused the Lord of bliss
>   to bear the dreadful curse for my soul.[6]

We can never fully comprehend God's immeasurable love for us. But we can, during this Lenten season, intentionally remember all of the ways that God has intentionally reached out in covenantal love to us through Noah, Abraham, Moses, and David—through the prophetic words of Jeremiah, and through the sacrificial love of Christ, who fulfills all of the covenants, exemplified in his life, death, and resurrection. And we know how God invites us to respond to that immeasurable, covenantal love. Pass it on. Live in the here and now with love inscribed on your heart. Forgive hurts incurred by others as God has forgiven you time and again. Live with the assurance that we can experience the richness of God's kingdom today and the fulfilment of the kingdom in the life to come. We can live fully now, and will live, because Jesus lives. We can follow without fear because we know where the journey will take us.

> *We can live fully now, and will live, because Jesus lives. We can follow without fear because we know where the journey will take us.*

May you experience the exultation that comes from knowing God has redeemed us—has redeemed *you*. God is never through with us. God's purpose will never be thwarted, no matter how much you and I may forget about God's great love and turn away. God's steadfast love will find a way and never stop until it has reached us, become part of us, and changed our hearts. Because God is a God who remembers. That is the covenant assurance we have from God.

ACKNOWLEDGMENTS

I had no idea, until those at Abingdon Press graciously agreed to publish my first book (and subsequent ones), how many people are involved, and the amount of work required, to bring a book to completion and make it available to readers. I also had no idea of the depth of gratitude my heart could hold for all of those people. So my first word of thanks is for you, the reader, for joining me on this Lenten journey.

Thank you for choosing this study and investing your time, heart, and soul in listening to what God has to say to you through each of the covenants God made through Noah, Abraham, Moses, and David. I pray that as you have delved into these covenants, that you have come to experience more fully the unfathomable love of God who never gives up on you, continually pursues relationship with you, always remembers you, and who laid down his life for you through the new covenant in Jesus Christ, the fulfillment of all of the covenants.

I am most grateful to Susan Salley, and my editor, Maria Mayo, at Abingdon Press, for inviting me to write a Lenten study, and saying "yes" to the idea of basing it on the God who remembers us and offers us redemption through covenants. I will be forever indebted to you both for your encouragement, guidance, and insights in bringing *Remember: God's Covenants and the Cross* to fruition, and for inviting me to Nashville to film the videos there with you.

A host of others on the Abingdon team were also invaluable in the production and publication of this book. To Randy Horick for the hours spent brainstorming with me the "what ifs" of each chapter, and for your beautiful writing skills tying the Leader Guide to the text and videos; to Tim Cobb for your meticulous work in laying out the book and walking it step by step through production; and to all at Abingdon Press who have made this book and study a reality, "thank you" seems inadequate, but it comes from the depths of my heart.

To the *numerous* crew at United Methodist Communications, who were responsible for the set design and production of the session videos, a *huge* thank you for your incredible hospitality, indefatigable energy and enthusiasm, and your professionalism and scrupulous attention to detail. The day spent with you, Brian Sigmon and Susan Salley, was pure joy!

To the Cox Chapel community of Highland Park United Methodist Church, deep gratitude to you for listening to the beginnings of this book that was born out of a Lenten sermon series prior to my retirement. And to the Highland Park UMC Women's Bible study, I am so blessed that you allowed me to teach the material for this book to you prior to its publication. The sharing of your questions, and your own stories, helped bring clarity and give shape to this book in more ways than you can know. I love you.

To Alice, Sue, Cindy, Beth, Fran, and Elizabeth, thank you for being sisters in covenant with me. Not only do you each reflect the deep covenantal love that God has for all people, the way in which you live your lives never lets me forget it.

Finally, to my husband, Ike, thank you for entering into the covenant of marriage with me thirty-five years ago, and for always taking that covenant seriously. I am grateful to you for your endless patience, support, and sacrificial love, and am grateful to God for you and the life we are blessed to share.

NOTES

Introduction

1. "Lighting of the Paschal Candle," *The United Methodist Book of Worship* (Nashville: The United Methodist Publishing House, 1992), 371

2. The readings from the Easter Vigil, and the congregational responses, may be found in *The United Methodist Book of Worship*, 373-375. Note that they don't all include the actual words of the covenants God makes, but they do reflect God's salvation and deliverance, and subsequent covenants made through Noah, Abraham, and Moses.

3. *The United Methodist Book of Worship*, 131.

4. "The Great Thanksgiving" from "Service of Word and Table I," *The United Methodist Book of Worship*, 36.

Chapter One. Noah: God's Covenant with Creation

1. Paraphrased from Genesis 3:19 and from "A Service for Ash Wednesday," *The United Methodist Book of Worship*, 323.

2. Monsignor Keith DeRouen, "19 things to give up for Lent that aren't chocolate." Daily World, February 20, 2018. https://www.dailyworld.com/story/opinion/2017/02/16/19-things-give-up-lent-arent-chocolate/98005614/.

Chapter Two. Abraham: A Promise of Nations

1. "Baptismal Covenant IV," *The United Methodist Book of Worship*, 112–113.

Chapter Three. Moses and Israel: Words of Life and Freedom

1. Leviticus 26:12 and Ezekiel 37:27 are Paul's sources for his quotation.

2. See *Words of Life: Jesus and the Promise of the Ten Commandments* (New York: Convergent Books, 2020).

3. See *Sabbath: Finding Rest, Renewal, and Delight in Our Busy Lives* (New York: Bantam Books, 2000).

4. *The Book of Common Prayer*, for the Episcopal Church (New York: Good Books, 2016), Proper 28. The Sunday closest to November 16, 205.
5. From a sermon by Dr. Roy Heller at Perkins School of Theology, Southern Methodist University, March 1, 2023
6. From sermon by Dr. Roy Heller, March 1, 2023.

Chapter Four. David: An Eternal Covenant

1. It is believed that the phrase "one fell swoop" may have originated with Shakespeare in *Macbeth* (Act IV, Scene 3) when he likens the murder of Macduff's wife and children to a hawk swooping down on defenseless prey.
2. Words recited at the imposing of ashes on Ash Wednesday, taken from Genesis 3:19.
3. Anna Quindlen, *A Short Guide to a Happy Life* (New York: Random House, 2000), 25–26.
4. Barbara Brown Taylor, "Dust to dust: The holiness of ashes." *The Christian Century*, March, 27, 2002, https://www.christiancentury .org/article/2002-03/dust-dust.
5. Barbara Brown Taylor. "Dust to dust: The holiness of ashes."

Chapter Five. From Jeremiah to Jesus: The Covenant of the Heart

1. Robert Robinson, "Come Thou Fount of Every Blessing," *The United Methodist Hymnal* (Nashville: The United Methodist Publishing House, 1989), 400, stanza 3.
2. St. Augustine of Hippo, *Confessions*, 1,1.5

Chapter Six. Jesus and the New Covenant

1. Some ancient authorities read "broken for," while others do not.
2. "The Man and the Birds Christmas Story," author unknown, as told by Paul Harvey, https://www.manandthebirds.com
3. Note that some ancient authorities do not contain the word "new," while others do (Matthew and Mark do not contain "new"). Mark and Luke omit "for the forgiveness of sins."
4. *The United Methodist Book of Worship*, 60.
5. *The United Methodist Book of Worship*, 61.
6. "What Wondrous Love Is This," USA folk hymn, *The United Methodist Hymnal*, 292, stanza 1.

Watch videos based on
Resurrection:
God's Covenants
and the Cross
with Susan Robb
through
Amplify Media.

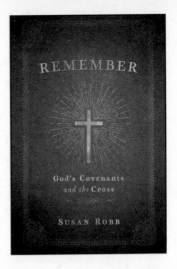

Amplify Media is a multimedia platform that delivers high quality, searchable content with an emphasis on Wesleyan perspectives for churchwide, group, or individual use on any device at any time. In a world of sometimes overwhelming choices, Amplify gives church leaders and congregants media capabilities that are contemporary, relevant, effective and, most importantly, affordable and sustainable.

With *Amplify Media* church leaders can:

- Provide a reliable source of Christian content through a Wesleyan lens for teaching, training, and inspiration in a customizable library
- Deliver their own preaching and worship content in a way the congregation knows and appreciates
- Build the church's capacity to innovate with engaging content and accessible technology
- Equip the congregation to better understand the Bible and its application
- Deepen discipleship beyond the church walls

**Ask your group leader or pastor about Amplify Media
and sign up today at www.AmplifyMedia.com.**